Finding Ullagundahi Island

FABIENNE BAYET-CHARLTON

ALLEN&UNWIN

First published in 2002

Australia Council for the Arts   Government of South Australia   A R T S A

This book has been assisted by the Commonwealth Government through
the Australia Council, its arts funding and advisory body, and by the
Government of South Australia through Arts South Australia.

Allen & Unwin
83 Alexander Street
Crows Nest NSW 2065
Australia
Phone: (61 2) 8425 0100
Fax: (61 2) 9906 2218
Email: info@allenandunwin.com
Web: www.allenandunwin.com

National Library of Australia
Cataloguing-in-Publication entry:

Bayet-Charlton, Fabienne.
   Finding Ullagundahi Island.

   ISBN 1 86508 586 3.

   1. Bayet-Charlton, Fabienne. 2. Aborigines, Australian—
Biography. 3. Aborigines, Australian—New South Wales.
I. Title.

305.89915

Set in 11/15.5 pt Scala by Asset Typesetting Pty Ltd
Printed in Australia by McPherson's Printing Group

10 9 8 7 6 5 4 3 2 1

To Simon,
with all my temperamental love

Author Note

Can I point out that, although this book is strongly autobiographical, it is not an autobiography. To be an autobiography everything in this book would have to be historically precise and that's not the case. I can say that just about every conversation recounted in the text happened. It's more the timing of events that have been adjusted.

And to be fair to my family, past work colleagues, friends and assorted characters I've met along the way I also need to say this book is from my perspective and I have written only what I have been able to see and say. I'm sure just about everybody in my family remembers my Nana differently as our own experiences, personalities and relationships with this wonderful woman differed. This book is not a claim to favouritism, special information or highly evolved wisdom. I'm biased and human. It's a story of dispossession if anything.

Contents

Soup

If I told you the truth of this story, like the marrow from the bones of oxtail soup, would you believe me? Would you accept only the soft, sticky tissue and suck it out, without the stock, through your teeth to loll on your tongue? Would you be satisfied with the marrow of a story, or would you wish for the garnish? Carrots and turnips floating around the edges half submerged. Cameo appearances. Are you really interested in the bones at all? Or are you just one of those people who relish the chewy bits? The slight exaggerations one makes when telling the gossip on Monday mornings.

So what if it's not the entire truth? A little bit of sauce won't hurt. What's a bit of flavour on the side? A bit of spice.

Are you one of those people? Do you forsake the marrow, the essence, the truth, for the vegetables? I do.

My mother, on the other hand, drools over any soup with bones in it and can handle any truth, no matter how brutal. She's that sort of woman. Oxtail soup, kangaroo soup, pea and ham soup. Any soup with bones in it. Any plot with truth in it.

$\mathcal{B}$ o n e s

To my mother the bones are the heart of soup. Truth is the heart of life.

She will sit at the table, pluck the bones from the bowl and suck the marrow with a moaning of contentment. She literally rejoices in the animalness of it. Then she will sop up the broth with her bread and at the end of the meal there will be a little mound of bones near the edge of her bowl. She will gather them and dump them into the bin with a sigh. All the while I will stare, slightly fascinated, slightly horrified, wondering . . .

I tried it once. To suck the marrow from the little cave of bone, but I found it so like the mucus that clots at the back of one's throat that I gagged and gave away the pleasure entirely to my mother. From then on I would only scoop the soup from the surface of the pot, letting the liquid seep over the sides of the ladle, seeking out the vegetables. I get to the story through the sauce. The blood.

Blood

Bone marrow is blood. Thick, red and rich, making the sauce for our dishes, for our stories. In the meat I used to notice small tubes and would cut them from their surrounding flesh and leave them on the edge of my plate. With time I realised that these tubes must have been connected to the rest of the once whole beast. Veins and arteries that trafficked the blood through its body. The beast's blood so like my own.

While these thoughts crossed my mind and subsequently my face—for I was never a child that could hide her thoughts—my mother spied on me. She watched her daughter change from herself, like some pagan ritual, alive and irreversible. I wonder what thoughts crossed her mind as this happened. I have never found out for, like a true mother, she had mastered the art of hiding her thoughts from her daughters. She is the marrow hiding in the bone.

We are different, my mother and I.

I've learned to hide myself as well. I've become a storyteller. I hide among the layers of life, fluid and murky. Perhaps I am the stock?

So I'm telling you this story and you will have to find me in the soup I'm about to cook.

1. Dolphin History

My Ashlyn May

This is to explain all that happened before you arrived in this world, into this sometimes-crazy family. This is to tell you who was here, why they had to go away, why it hurt so much and why your unexpected arrival caused so much joy, so much confusion. Let's face it, you were not expected.

I have tried to tell you this before but you just fall asleep. Your dad gazes down, breathing in the smell of baby. Frog-like smirk: 'Jeez, she's a good kid.' You keep sleeping, softly wriggling as if to confirm your innocence. I guess this is to be expected as you are only four weeks old. Your eyelids droop and close and you are whisked away to dream land. If only I could follow and talk there, during dreams. Your story is about your Dreaming, before your life. Before this time.

I want to tell you about Nana, Mabel Louise Freeburn, about where she came from and where she is now, because, in a sense, that is where you are from, at least in your blood. When you visit places you will know why they exist and how they came to be and how you can have a feeling, a familiarity, about people without even trying. Without even waking up from your dreams.

You would have loved Nana. Why? Because you wouldn't have been able to help yourself. I'm not just biased. You ask anyone who knew her. She had a way of weaving love and warmth into everything, diffusing through everybody she met. Like soft warm water easing over your skin and the sun warm on your back. Enough of these sensations, we can talk about them later. When you discover life for itself. 'Slowly, slowly,' your dad says. Slowly slowly.

But that's my trouble. I'm in too much of a hurry. To tell you all about our family and our past and all the things that you have to look forward to. Love, food, forests, the sea, rivers, and the dust of the desert. When awake your eyes search for colour, movement. Look to the sky. See the rosellas, clashing red with the green of the trees. Already your mouth tastes milk. Your little fingers grasp, your growing arms and legs force open the swaddling, kicking and gesticulating in the air.

Nothing will hold you back, I know, but in the meantime I need to get this down before it's too late.

Before this fades from my memory and turns to the dust found at the bottom of kitchen cupboards or behind the rusted tools at the back of the shed. I just don't have the patience. How long do I have to wait for you to read? Slowly, slowly.

So, Ashlyn, this is how it begins and ends with you.

$\mathcal{B}us$

Head jerks awake. What am I doing here? I'm on a bus. Stinking, stale smell. Gritty, sticky seats. The atmosphere is turgid with resignation. It's seven in the morning, clouds overhead threaten to soak the city in grey. It's cold. In temperature and feeling. Perched up behind the balding bus driver. He tries conversation.

'So, you a Sydney girl, hey?' Face grimacing into a smile. Neck creaking around.

'No, I'm from Adelaide.' Polite smile. Veneer hides the thoughts. And don't call me girl, moron.

'Adelaide, aye?'

Keep your eyes on the road.

Lips press together. Smile thinning. Wanna make something of it?

'What's a small-town girl like you doing in the big smoke?' he leers.

'Research actually. I work for the Parliamentary Research Service in Canberra.' It's a lie. Used to. Quit last week. That should shut him up. And it does. Neck cricks back to the road. The bus rumbles through the traffic. Oil shimmers on his hair, down his neck.

'Where ya heading?' This question alarms. Shouldn't he know? He's the driver.

'Grafton.' Search for another seat. Eyes scan the back of the bus. Too full.

'Whadya wanna go to Grafton for?' He's irritable now. 'It's just a glorified truck stop.' The bus veers dangerously towards the road dividers. Bump, bump, bump. He finally concentrates. End of conversation.

Looking out of the window. The cold mists the view. I take pictures of the Harbour Bridge. They won't come out. It doesn't matter. It's not to see them; it's purely a mechanical thing. I'm not seeing what I'm looking at anyway. I'm remembering . . .

Backyard Dreamtime

In my mind I'm looking out over a garden, where the sun is a bright orange and the sand at my feet hot red. Insects are buzzing. I'm with Nana. We are sitting in a garden a long time ago. A lifetime ago. Sitting, watching the day go past. Talking about good times, family times and plans for the future. We are talking about my university study, in another cold and grey city.

And Nana is saying, 'You know, Fab, it's good that

you're doing this course, learning about our people, because we've lost our culture. We weren't allowed to talk about our people, our past.'

I nod and stare at the flowers, too happy to look at Nana. Too proud. We sit for a while, then make another cuppa. Two tea bags in Nana's cup—she likes it strong. You can stand your spoon up in it. But no sugar. Sugar is bad for the diabetes. Nana gave up sugar ages ago, but never tea. She'd never give up her cuppa tea. Or her smokes. We sit lazy in the warm sun, wrapped in the warm air, just admiring the beautiful flowers. Nana sits under the shade, near the tank stand, so she doesn't get too hot. I sit in the full glare of the sun, squinting, desperately trying to get some of my tan back, lost since living in the city. Trying to get some of my 'Aboriginality' back.

Teasing uncles say, 'Hey, Fab, where's your colour? Aren't you gonna be black any more? You bleaching yourself like Michael Jackson? You lookin' a bit pale there, Fab. You sick or something?' They guffaw into their beards, thump each other on the back. 'Man oh man,' they say. Brothers in arms.

'I'll show them. I'll tan in five minutes flat, they'll see,' I think vainly to myself. 'And all my uncles will be dazzled by my colour, my gorgeous good looks.' But I never do. Only my nose goes bright red and the rest of my face looks as pale as before. White-woman-wannabe. Black on the inside. Nana just chuckles.

We sit a long time in that garden. We talk for a long time, like we always did, sitting there watching the morning go by, waiting for the 'Midday Show' on TV, while everybody else is out. It's just Nana and I, talking about life, just talking about everything and nothing.

But like fat bubbles rising to the surface of a creek bed when you squish the red mud with your toes, like a big, full bubble rising unstoppably through murky brown water, I have to ask a stupid question.

'Hey Nana. How come you never talk about where you come from? Did something bad happen to you? How come? But if you don't wanna talk about it . . . it's alright, you know . . . but I was just wondering . . .' Real casual like . . . about as casual as a bullock stepping on waterlilies.

'Oh, now I've stuffed it,' I think.

Nana has never spoken about where she comes from. It's like there's this family taboo about it. If Nana doesn't want to talk about it, don't push her. There are bad memories there. So let it go. Don't go stirring the mud of the past. Don't go raising any bubbles.

I've broken a major rule and now I'm in for it. But we've all wanted to know for years where we really come from. We all want to know why, after being born in New South Wales (which seems like the other side of the world to me), we have ended up in the middle of Australia, the desert, Coober Pedy.

Uncle Mark has tried for years to get Nana to talk

about her past, about her childhood. 'Go on, Mum, tell us. Tell us the old stories, the stories of us kids, like we do Christmas time, with a couple of beers, around the table.' But Nana won't.

So I'm staring at the flowers in the garden. Too afraid to look left or right, waiting to see if Nana is going to answer.

And softly, quietly, so as not to wake old feelings, and maybe old spirits, Nana speaks about her life, about her family, her childhood, before the desert. She talks of her home, the strength of her childhood. She tells me about a river so wide, blue and meandering that her people lived in the middle of it, and trees so dense in numbers, so thick with leaves, they created a canopy of green mist throughout the land.

I sit there with my feet planted in the acrid red dust, looking into my pale tea. Not believing.

'But how, Nana? How could a river be so wide that people could live on it? I mean, you look at the Torrens down in Adelaide, they call that a river but it's just a muddy duck pond. And you look at the Murray, now that's a bloody big river, but it's not blue, is it? No, it's about the colour of your cuppa tea there, Nana, and in some places it looks like chocolate milkshake.'

It churns rather than flows, I think to myself. Nothing can live in a river like that, 'cept maybe spirits. I don't want to think about that. Better to steer clear of what you can't see.

'How can people live on a river, Nana? Like it's land? How can a river be *that* big.'

Nana eyed me up and down, like a wise old turtle.

'Because it is.' She sighs, sips her tea and says nothing more.

It was a lifetime ago. We sat together in that garden of red sand with its defiant little plants raising their flowers to burn in the sun.

And now, well now, I'm on this bus, my nose smearing skin grease on the window, out looking for a river. Stickybeaking like some bloody loud-shirted-tourist-cum-anthropologist. I have to know how a river could be so wide, so blue, so thick with life, that it could nurture a whole community of people, a whole lifetime of memories. The bus lurches about the road. I glare at the back of the bus driver's head. He has a few thin strands of hair oiled across a bare patch. I will it to bald faster.

'Why am I doing this?' I ask myself again. I search for voices within. Guidance from ancestors perhaps? But there's no answer.

Bundjalung Rain

Dead silence.

Dry flat featureless land.

No sound, no noise, perhaps a breeze to stir the dust,

wafting, soft in the air. Silence. Like being in a vacuum, only hearing the heartbeat, the rushing of blood across translucent eardrums. Imagine that.

Then it rained. The first droplets spotting the dust. Then a slow increase in tempo, drumming. Then bucketing down.

It just rained and rained. Pouring thick dollops of wet on everything.

Blue-grey rain, blackening the parched red earth, filling it with moisture, with life.

The dust writhed under the moisture, at first sucking it up like a sponge. Drinking. The dust settled. Grateful, it waited for the rain to stop.

Clay

Then the dust became saturated and uncomfortable, heavy under the weight of so much water. It turned to mud, then clay, writhing, swirling and darkening like thick chocolate. The novelty of the rain began to wear. The dust wanted to shake off the wet, the cold. It craved its original lightness, to float with the breeze, the silence of the wind. The clay hurt from the constant slapping of the rain.

The clay pressed closer together, pushing out the water. It heaved and groaned. In the separation of forces it changed the features of the land. The land, soaked and sponge-like, pushed its water out to form the rivers, to form the mountains, the valleys at first smooth and bare. The land was bloodletting. Waiting for its people.

The people began to emerge, groaning and aching with the wet. Dark people, built of dust, formed by water, shaped by the wind. They clawed their way from the earth. They pulled each other up from the dust, from the valleys, from the mountains. Holding on to each other. They sought shelter from the rain. They looked for the warmth of the sun and so seeking it the sun was born. Upon their gaze trees rose from the earth's shoulders. They craved the tranquillity of the stars and with their desire the night was created. Men and women of clay. Thick, strong, sinuous clay. Black clay.

These people looked to live, and through their defining of life they shaped the earth. They arrived in this land and at the same time they created this land. Just as the land had created them. Through their actions and lives the land took shape and meaning. They were the ancestors.

There are those who believe we were born of this land, and those who say we were the first migrants. Either way it is the same, the first touch between flesh and soil, the first markings. It is what defines humans from animals. This land is so old. She has infinite patience. She can wait for people to come. She can create them from the folds of her skin . . .

With such creation the Dreaming had begun . . .

In the rising of the first sun to warm the rain-drenched earth, three brothers sailed from the east. These brothers bore various names, depending on who you believe and what language you speak. Some have written their names as Berrung, Mommon and Yaburong. But don't ask me to say them, I cannot remember my language . . .

These brothers sailed with their families towards our land. From a distance the land looked lush and green. The mountains blurred the horizon in purple hues. Or was it the clouds that played tricks on their eyes? Their canoes moved closer to the land but they could see only the salt-encrusted coast, pale with sand, studded with cliffs and boulders. The green promise of forest was only an illusion. Despondently they moved away, thirsting for fresh water, cool land.

From a cliff a woman with skin the colour of clay called out to the sailors, inviting them to her land, to stay. She called out to them but they did not hear her and against the dark landscape they could not see her. She called to them again and again but the three brothers and their canoes moved away.

Frustrated, the clay woman called out to the sea. She bade the sea wreck the seafarers and bring them to land. The canoes broke apart with the rising of the waves and smashed against the boulders, staining them black. Large pieces solidified into jutting rocks. Shredded wood sank to the sea floor and transformed into seagrass. Berrung, Mommon, Yaburong and their families were forced to swim. The women held their babies above them. Lost and exhausted they beached themselves upon the shore.

With that, the woman of clay turned from the sea and walked inland, towards the forest and mountains.

The travellers huddled together on the sand. The women comforted their babies while the men planned to look for materials to build canoes. Others organised to search for food. A woman broke from the group on the beach and began to walk alone.

Yams

Dirrangun, one of the old women with many daughters and grandchildren, walked along the water's edge for a while, then headed inland, beyond the salty, spindly shrubs, over the dunes. She sought peace, away from the constant wind, the never-ending rush of the waves.

The gritty sand gradually turned softer and brown under her feet. The sinewy trees of the coast shed their salt and turned lush and green with each step Dirrangun took. The land opened to her and began to offer her the forest. Trees tall and wet. Mist hung green and silent. Sighing to the ground Dirrangun began to dig for yams. The moist soil crusted under her nails as she dug and her body ached with the effort of surviving the sea. She longed to rest under the trees.

Her family would be waiting, hungry. She was pleased with the food she had found. Dirrangun gathered the yams in her arms and turned back towards the beach. The woman of clay appeared in front of her. Dirrangun dropped her harvest. The woman gestured to calm her and said, 'You are my sister now. The soil from which you feed is your home. You are welcome to stay.'

Dirrangun sighed with relief. Her long hair was turning grey with years and she was weary of the sea. Other clay people emerged from the mists, dark people but not sombre, and she saw that their faces mirrored her own. Dirrangun felt the soil stain her skin and decided her family should stay in this new place.

She turned back to the beach to tell her family they had found home.

But while she was gone, the sun had peaked. Berrung, Mommon and Yaburong had eaten fish and mussels. Their bellies were full. They had found enough wood to create new canoes. They sealed the canoes with sap from fire.

They looked to where Dirrangun had walked and saw only the salt-encrusted coast. They reasoned that Dirrangun must have perished, being so old. The three brothers convinced their families to leave without her.

The camp fires had settled to embers and the brothers were impatient to move.

As her people sailed from the coast Dirrangun returned to the camp. She called out to the brothers, urging them to turn back. Weeping with dismay she called out to them again and again. Still they would not turn back. Her disappointment turned to anger, and clenching her fists, she cursed her family. As her tears fell to the sand and mixed with the water the sea began to turn violent. Waves thrashed into a storm and again the seafarers were forced to land, only this time further up the coast. With that, Dirrangun consoled herself by setting up camp in the forest and living on yams. She named her new camp Yamba.

Once her family had settled they came looking for Dirrangun and she introduced her family to the people of clay. The three brothers created clans with the clay people and moved north, south and west from the east and from Yamba. Together, over time, they peopled the forests, rivers and coasts. They all looked to Dirrangun who had united them.

But Dirrangun had not forgotten the sense of rejection she felt when her family tried to sail away without her. From then on she remained very wary of her family and lived away from them. As Dirrangun became older and more vulnerable she began to hide her food and water.

The dust of time started to weigh Dirrangun down

and turn her skin grey. Her long hair turned white and formed a halo around her face. People began to believe Dirrangun was part spirit. Only the old clay woman became her friend, teaching her to spirit herself away in the forest.

Dirrangun moved inland, up into the mountains where the forest canopy shut out the light. She stayed at the base of a spring and kept it hidden under some bracken. Two of Dirrangun's daughters needed somewhere to stay and Dirrangun made them welcome. But after a while the good feeling between the women began to wane and they argued. One of the sisters' husbands intervened. As a husband he had the title of buloogan. He was a handsome, almost arrogant man. He had forgotten the importance of Dirrangun and saw only an old stick of a woman. He ridiculed Dirrangun and would not allow her any food. Dirrangun hid her water and waited for these youngsters to leave. But they didn't leave and just fell asleep at her camp.

While everyone was sleeping, two of the buloogan's dogs found the hidden spring. Snuffling the bracken away the dogs slurped up the water. Happy and dripping water they ran to their master and licked him on the face. The buloogan awoke and followed the trail of water back to the spring. Dirrangun lay curled around it.

Angry at being outsmarted by an old woman the buloogan thrust his spear into the spring, fracturing the rocks around it. The water burst through, forcing

Dirrangun away. Full of pride and arrogant with his new power, the buloogan called to the water to drown Dirrangun. Although Dirrangun tried to build a platform above the rising water, it swept her and the trees away. Dirrangun tried to push mountains to dam the spring but the water just flowed over and around them. Forests submerged under the water and the people fled to higher ground.

The force of the water from the fractured spring caused the valleys to flood, leaving hundreds of islands in its wake. This became the Clarence River.

Dirrangun tried to sit in the floodwaters and use her powers to block the flow but the river proved too strong for her and she was pushed out of the way. Helpless and angry she stood at Yamba and watched as the fresh water washed into the sea.

Betrayed by her family again, Dirrangun threw herself, angry and despairing, into the water. Her white hair dissolved into foam. Knowing she had lost her spring forever, Dirrangun cursed the river to turn salty so no one could drink it near her old resting place. The water around her churned, salty and bitter. Her body turned to stone. Where the river meets the sea.

Whenever you hear the roaring of the ocean and see the foam, bitter and frothing on the beach, that's Dirrangun making sure no one can drink her water. It is Dirrangun in despair. It is Dirrangun's Dreaming.

The Dreaming hasn't stopped.

The bus lurches to a stop.

I peer out of the window. Pouring rain. Out in the murk glows a yellowing service station. Through the black an occasional light flickers and passes. Apart from that there is nothing. Not a figure. Maybe Grafton *is* literally a truckies' stop. This can't be Grafton. Nana told me about Grafton.

'It's a beautiful, big town. Jacarandas bloom purple down the main street. It's on the river. We used to travel there when I was a girl. They used to hold a market in the town square every Sunday.

'Just stop there and ask anybody about the island. Everybody will know where it is. Just say, "I'm looking for Ullagundahi Island," and you'll get directions clear as day. It's just between Grafton and Maclean. You can't miss it.'

It looks as though I've missed it.

'This stop, Grafton,' yells the bus driver. He grins. There's malice in that smile. Bastard was right.

I get up. Where am I going to sleep? I won't be able to camp in this downpour. I haven't ever imagined that it would rain this hard in Australia. Surely everybody's been swept away by now. I look around. Nobody seems unduly alarmed, even those getting off the bus.

'Anybody meeting you?' Leering bus driver. Eyebrows raised suggestively.

'Oh, yes. My great-uncle should be here.'

Great-uncle? I know I have a great-uncle somewhere in Grafton, but he doesn't know I'm coming. Only met him once or twice before . . .

'Can't see him anywhere,' as if he knows I am lying.

'I expect he'll be waiting inside. Thank you for a lovely drive.' Cringe.

Why did I have to say that? Why do I have to be polite to utter gits? I paid for the fare.

Confidence slipping. What am I doing here?

The distance from the bus to the petrol station is only five metres but by the time I reach the door I'm soaked. Hair dripping. I can feel rivulets of water down my back, pooling into my underwear. I look at my backpack. Nothing would be dry in there. Why the hell did I bring a backpack? Only foreigners travel with backpacks. When Australians travel they carry suitcases, or carry bags, or big-striped plastic bags, and pillows. I didn't even bring a pillow. Stupid, stupid. Push the greasy doors. At least it's dry inside. No other passengers bother to come in; they've all been met under the verandah. Two attendants stand behind the hot-chip counter. Dressed identically in the yellow of the petrol station. Occasional coffee stain. They look up expectantly. One holds her chip tongs at the ready. Their round faces glow yellow from the neon light.

They think I'm a European tourist. You can tell just by looking at their faces. They'll be disappointed as soon as I open my mouth.

Sodden, embarrassed, I slush up to the counter.

'Is this Grafton?' Their faces drop immediately. The one with the tongs stabs at the chips viciously. So much for the glamour of travel.

'Yeah, this is Grafton.'

The other rallies. 'Can I help you?'

'Is this Grafton? What I mean to say is, well . . . is that all of Grafton . . . outside.' Water sprays from my hand and lands on the chip counter. They both stare. The drips evaporate, leaving tiny tide marks. The yellow twins look at each other.

Eventually the helpful one says, 'Yeah, that's Grafton outside.'

'Where's the river?'

'The river?'

'Do you know?'

'Just down the road.'

'How far?'

'Coupla ks. Can't miss it,' says the one with the tongs.

'And Grafton? Is this Grafton?'

'Yeah, but most of the township is on the other side.'

This is firmer ground. 'Okay.' Now we're getting somewhere, I'm thinking, taking a deep breath. 'Do you know where Ullagundahi Island is?'

The yellow twins look at me as if I'm an alien.

'What?'

'Ullagundahi Island.'

The twins look at each other again. I imagine their thoughts: 'This here's a strange one.'

'Never heard of it.'

'It's an island in the middle of the Clarence River. Do you know where it is?' I'm getting desperate now. Maybe Nana had her rivers mixed up? No, how could that have happened, she had lived on it for Christ's sake.

I try again. 'The river down the road, that is the Clarence River, isn't it?'

'Yeah, it's the Clarence.'

'Well, there's an island in the middle of it, isn't there?'

The helpful one says, 'Miss, there's over three hundred islands in the Clarence River.'

A pause. A tremor. A pulse. My heart squeezes. Just once. It throbs in my eardrums and I feel as though it can be heard across this continent and felt in the dust of the desert. The floor swells like a wave beneath me, then settles. The helpful attendant is still talking . . .

'Though I've never heard of one called Ullagundahi. Not round Grafton anyway.' The other attendant is eating the chips. No one else is going to be in tonight.

'Would you like a map of the area? There's some lovely sights around. There's a wildlife sanctuary just

out of Grafton, with koalas and kangaroos and . . .
I think it's got an emu . . .' She turns. 'Tom's still got
on an emu, hasn't he?'

The other shrugs her shoulders and continues
eating, greasy and bloated in her uniform.

'I'll just have a coffee . . . thanks.'

Black and strong and as bitter as my mood. I hand
over some wet money. The yellow twins happily busy
themselves finding the polystyrene cups. One holds it.
The other pours.

I have to ring Nana. She didn't tell me about this.

Cold fingers slip on the numbers. 'Please, please
let someone be home.' I think of all the other places
they could be. No one will be home. Maybe they've
gone camping, gone to the pub . . . Maybe they've gone
shopping . . . No, it is night-time . . . Press the receiver
to wet hair. The mouthpiece smells of stale chips.

Please let me speak to Nana. Bruno answers the
phone.

'Bruno, can I speak to Nana? It's Fab. I'm ringing
from Grafton . . . New South Wales. What am I doing
here? I'm ringing from a public phone . . . Yes, Bruno
. . . and I haven't got much money. She's resting?
Is she asleep? Can she come to the phone? No? Okay,
thanks, Bruno.'

I hang up and turn back to the counter.

The twins present a fresh polystyrene cup, beaming
to be of assistance.

'Perhaps you should ask someone at Yamba.'
'Yamba? Where the hell is Yamba?'

Yamba

If you look for Yamba on most maps of Australia you won't find it, because it won't be there. Its existence depends on its importance to the person seeking it, but if you live there then it's bloody important and you'd better not forget to write it down on those bureaucratic maps of yours mate, or else.

If you fly over Yamba, in a small one-engine plane, cavorting wildly up and down on the steps of the summer thermals, bump, bump, you can see that Yamba is crouched on the edge of the world. Squeezed in beside a wide meandering green river and the beautiful turquoise sea.

Place a little dot on the eastern edge of the continent, just next to that meandering river, just between sea and land.

The sea laps casually at the mainland, like a mistress petting her favourite dog.

Land

Land is the remaining boundary of Yamba. Lush green forested land. Grazing land. Sugarcane land. Land you could grow anything on, almost by mistake. You could spit melon seeds into this land on your birthday and they would come up all by themselves by Christmas. The best we can do to this land is nothing. Walk away from this land and let it grow, abundant, lush and green, like the rainforest that once covered it. But we humans, we worry about land.

We cut it. We clear it, burn it, saturate it with insecticides, pesticides and fertilisers. We inject it with everything imaginable, like steroids into muscle. We put strange animals on it, we strip animals from it. We herd people off it and stake strangers upon it. We dig into it, drill it with holes, fill the holes up. We drive on it, tar it, water it, dry it out, live on it, sleep on it. (We don't shit on it. The shit goes into the crystal clear water.) And amongst all of this we hold conferences. We legislate about it, we publish papers about it. We use the land. We worry about the land.

And the land does its best to ignore us.

$\mathcal{S}ea$

The people of Yamba try to ignore the land. They are fishing people. They are typical of humans. There is a collective dreaming amongst us regardless of race or culture. We all have a thirsting for the undrinkable, the impossible sea. We crouch on the edge of the continent and gaze out. We dream of living on the sea's blue surface, walking over the blue. There is a craving for the constant wet that burns our skin, the salt that chafes us to our bones. We live on the most beautiful land in the world, yet most of us turn our backs on it and watch the turquoise horizon, enraptured and in love, yearning for acceptance. Unrequited love, like the first impossible crush.

You know it is impossible because the sea doesn't even know you exist. And if she did, if you could attract her attention for just a second, just a moment as you wallow hopelessly in the shallows of her waves, her presence, head back, floating on the surface, arms waving for assistance, bravely smiling, bravely believing that she, the love of your dreams, will rescue you, accept you or change you into something that can live in her world, she throws you against the rocks. She pulls you into her rip, hidden beneath the demure ripples, her playful absent-minded waves. With the flick of a wrist she drowns you. The sea immense. And not one of us ever learns. We are bewitched by her horizon. When we cannot see her we are miserable.

So, as far as the people of Yamba are concerned, they are waterlocked into the land. The river flows silent, serpentine, beside them, leading them into the sea. The sea is their front porch, their parlour, where they take their friends to entertain. The land behind them, the entire mutilated yet beautiful continent, is merely a concession to the fact that we humans cannot walk on water.

Yamba, with its quiet but prosperous main street. Six fish and chip shops. You want fresh fruit and veg? Move inland. 'The key to paradise here, mate, is a fishing rod and, if you're rich, a boat. Yes, the key is a boat.'

A sticker in the main shop heralds, 'Those who don't know how to fish, work.'

So you come to Yamba. Small crouching Yamba, with its blue and white shacks, its tidy town rows (meandering to the curves of the river). Yamba is where the river meets the sea. It is the edge of the world for some and the beginning of the world for others. And the locals say, 'If you know Yamba,' with a conspiring wink and leer, sweat crusted with the salt and sand of the ocean, 'if you know where to go and what's what, mate, then you can see the edge of the world.' Especially while having a few beers at the local pub.

'Just turn right at the white lighthouse.' Starched white, straight and tall. Like a priest's penis, guiding lost fishermen to the salvation and boring redemption of the land after a night with their mistress the sea. Just beyond there, perched high on the edge of the cliff where a woman of legend once stood, poised, as if ready to dive into the sea below, is the pub. Quite normal on the outside. Far more comforting in the light of day than the stark white lighthouse. Fading paint, haphazard extensions over the years. The old airconditioner rattling away, almost ready to fall from the wall, propped up by a broomstick. Propped up like the locals along the bar.

Inside. Once your eyes have adjusted to the customary dark interior and the smell of smoke, beer, stale salt and vinegar chips crushed into the orange and brown paisley carpet, the comfortable dinginess of the place, you can see from the other side of the front bar the edge of the world. The hypnotic sea.

So you order your beer as nonchalantly as you can, all the time staring past the bartender's head into the blue behind him. You pay the fifty cents surcharge because, 'You're not a regular drinker round here, are you?' The bartender can see that. You ask as discreetly, as intimately as possible, how to get to the ladies' lounge where the godforsaken enormous window is. Where just that membrane of glass splits the continent from the sea like the strip of beach below. The bartender,

bored by now, suggests, 'Round the bar. There is a
door marked "Ladies' Lounge" . . . You can't miss it.'
You've now confirmed to him that you're a tourist
and he realises he could've taken you for a lot more than
fifty cents.

You swagger to the window, as slowly as you can.
Beer in hand, salt and vinegar chips in the other. You
pretend to be a local, you let your hips do the walking.
You are safe to sit . . . until the next beer. See the edge
of the world.

Blue and White

Everything is blue and white here. The sea, so many
waves of blue. Like the bleeding of paint into paper
they wash into each other. Wide sweeping sopping
brushstrokes, layering upon one another, seeping into
each other, yet clear and shallow. Merely an optical
illusion. Thick white scrapings of foam, frothing,
opaque against the translucent blue. The edges continue the story of conflict between land and sea. Who
shall win? Neither, in this unwanted union that gives
birth to foam, frothing forth, fading, then bubbling
again. The blue sky is so bright as to fade everything
under it. All looks worn, bleached and old. White
clouds wisping like strands of cotton.

'The colour is fading from my eyes.' I've started

talking to myself. 'I need another beer.' Back to the bar and I wonder if it's worth asking the bartender about Ullagundahi but the disaster at the service station keeps my mouth shut. I imagine opening the conversation, 'I'm looking for an island . . .'

'We're all looking for something, love.'

'Oh yeah . . .'

Oh no . . . Maybe after this drink. I scurry back to my table and keep looking out to the edge of the world.

The rest of it—the people walking on the sickle beach; the pale orange sand, shells encrusted on the black rocks; and the pool that some man has carved from rocks that purges with each tide—is mere detail, hardly worth noticing. But I do.

In my mind, swirling with beer, I see an old man. He's sitting on a mission reserve, perhaps on the steps of his tin hut. I can see the mud freshly drying and crusting in the morning sun. The old man is sitting, smoking. Beside him, madly scribbling, is an anthropologist. His eyes and ears gobble up every word the old man says . . .

Greedy Man

'Back in the old days there used to be dolphins. Dolphins were my people's friends. They were our brothers. We all used to camp up in the mountains

34

when it was winter, sleep in the caves, warm by the fire . . .

'Anyways, we used to be up there eating good tucker. Fat with possums, wallaby, you name it, there was plenty. Plenty for everyone . . . not like now.'

'Possums, you say?'

'Yeah, possums, echidnas, good feeds, good tucker. Not like beef, softer, not stringy . . .

'We used to sit in the camp with our elders and the others would come down when the fish were on the run . . . The elders would know when the fish would be ready, by the flowers, the seasons, the sun, you know. The old people knew.

'They'd all go down to the river, they could feel the fish swimming through the water. A whole mob of them . . . the river would be full of fish. Then, when everybody was down there, they would get together and beat their spears and coolamons on the water. They'd be calling out to the dolphins. See? They'd be calling them to round them fish up. The men would beat for the dolphins to come and the women would walk with the nets in the water. The dolphins would come and chase those fish into the nets. That way the old people would catch a big mob of fish. They'd scoop them up with their nets and everybody would share.'

'What sort of fish?'

'Oh you know, they've got different names now. Go and ask those government blokes, they'd know . . .'

'So you're saying the dolphins were the people's friends?'

'The dolphins used to protect our people from the sharks. When we wanted to cross the river the old people would call out to the dolphins to protect us. Do that out on the beach too. Used to be. In the olden days . . .

'But then there was this greedy fella. He wanted all the fish to himself. Him and his mate called out to the dolphins to help them. The dolphins came, they were like our blood, but this greedy fella decided to catch one in his net. He wanted to see why the dolphins were so smart. He caught this dolphin and killed it with his wadi. The other dolphins could see their kin's blood in the water and swam away from the danger. The greedy fella dragged the dolphin's body onto the beach and cut it open to find its brains. He was trying to find the dolphin's spirit and make it his own. He was breaking the sacred law. The other fella saw what he was doing and ran away.

'A few days after this the people came down to catch fish and called to the dolphins. The dolphins would not come. The men beat on the water and the women sang out, holding their nets, waiting. But the dolphins stayed away. No fish were caught that day and the people went home hungry. They sat around and wondered what was the matter. People couldn't cross the river because they were frightened without the dolphins. They thought the river might've been angry. The people called a meeting with the elders and told them about the dolphins.

'The old people sat and talked together. Pretty soon the fella who had seen the dolphin being killed owned up and told the elders about that greedy fella. They hunted the greedy fella down and killed him with a wadi, the same way he had killed the dolphin. They took his body and threw him into the sea as a way of saying sorry. But throwing him into the sea did no good. The dolphins weren't as friendly any more. They kept an eye on us because they are our kin, but they kept their distance from us too—the trust was gone. The people would have to learn to fish on their own . . . all because of that greedy fella.'

Sugar

The anthropologist gobbles the black man's words. He pays him with food, some sugared biscuits perhaps. He leaves the man sitting on the steps of his shack. The exchange will not sit well in their stomachs. The anthropologist will spew the words back out onto paper. He will publish his findings. He will be attacked by other anthropologists for not being scientific, not being real. His stomach will turn bitter with shame, disappointment. The old man will eat his biscuits and aggravate his diabetes, maybe suffer kidney failure . . .

Hear the old man talking in the sun. Perhaps it was fifty years ago, maybe a hundred. Perhaps it was yesterday. It is the same.

The Edge of the World

I almost forget that I'm one of the drinkers, sitting in this pub at Yamba. I'm looking out the window over the edge of the world and I think, 'I am not a person. I am a slash of blue. A colour, fading . . .' I'm deluding myself that I am part of the sea. That I can see everything.

When really I can see nothing.

I'd better try Nana again. I need to talk to her before I get too drunk.

Phone Call

She's there on the other end of the line and everything eases as I tell her where I am.

'Oh, Yamba.' Nana is speaking about an old friend she visited only yesterday. She sighed, 'It's beautiful, isn't it?'

'Yes, it's just how you described it, Nana.'

'Does Yamba still have the lighthouse?'

'Yes, Nana.'

'Did you go to the cliffs?'

'Yep.'

'Does it still have the fishing boats?'

'Yes.'

'And the reeds along the river?'

'Hmmm, not sure.'

'Nana?'

'Hmmm?'

'I'm seeing . . . things.'

'What things, Fab?'

I want to tell her about the water, about the trees. How there are so many colours of blue and other things. But I don't know how to say it. I can't find the right words.

'Oh, I saw this boat with your name on it, Nana.'

'Did you now?' Nana's tone has changed, she has her guard up, but I don't know why and I ramble on.

'Yeah, it was called *Freeburn*, and it was in the reeds and it was painted in blue and white stripes and—'

But Nana interrupts me.

'It's where the river meets the sea, Fab,' Nana says.

'Yes.'

'It's where the dolphins came from.'

'Yes, Nana.'

'. . . beautiful Yamba.' The phone beeps in alarm as it runs out of money. 'Talk to me soon, Fub.'

39

'Yep, Nana. I will.'

I hang up—fucking Telstra—and walk back to the table next to the window. Shove away the beer.

My Ashlyn May

I did mean to talk to Nana again. But she was thousands of miles away, far inland, beyond this land of watermelon pips, rivers and cane fields. Far away from her memories and her childhood.

Nana was where I began my life, my memories. She was in the landscape of my childhood, my Dreaming.

Until I woke up.

And how did I wake up, my Ashlyn May? With an opening of my eyes.

2. Coober Pedy
Twilight

Blink Blink

Blink blink. I'm awake. It's day but it is still dark. I'm alone in this cavern that is my Nana's bedroom. Deep underground, under dirt, under rock. All I see is black but if I keep my eyes open for a while the light seeps through. Pale, powdery.

And the air is flavoured with dust and the smell of talcum powder. Johnson & Johnson. I'm in the tiny bed near the corner of the room, almost behind a narrow white wardrobe. The rock ceiling rounds above me like a womb. The shaft from the roof opens wide, yet I'm shaded by the old forty-four gallon drum on the hill. Light wafts down, soft, dusty. The walls of the room begin to glow a soft purple-pink. Like bruised flesh, but it's friendly because it's hiding me away from the rest of the world. It is keeping me safe and warm because

43

I am tiny and alone. My hands try to grasp out in front of me. Fingers uncurl like flimsy green leaves.

Across the room stands Nana's fat queen-sized bed. It puffs at me with its three layers of mattress added over the years. With the pale towelling bedspread it glows benignly, like an enormous wedding cake, in the dim. If I sit on it the marshmallow deflates and I am left stranded in the middle. Soft, it takes my weight and folds in on me.

There is barely walking space between the bed and the narrow white wardrobe on one side, and the rough wooden bench on the other. Squatting between the bed and bench is a tiny wooden table, painted dark brown. On it, a single lamp. No lampshade.

The bed is empty. Nana got up hours ago.

But I'm in this bed with my stick-like bones and goose-pimpled skin. It is like a cot, with a spare sheet, a foam mattress and old flattened pillows. I wriggle down into the warmth. The blanket untucks and creeps up my legs, leaving my ankles exposed to the cool dark. If I move, my toes will stub against the sand-patterned walls my body has snuggled up towards during the night. Already veins of gypsum glow in the light pouring down the shaft. It is cool and dark down here. It is safe. Above the bed someone has written 'Heaven' on the wall. It has begun to hide under dust.

I turn my head and am momentarily blinded. There is a long narrow passage leading away into the light.

There is a muffled clatter. Cutlery. The radio is on. A kettle begins to whistle, wheezy at first. The smell of food pushes its way down the passage. My mouth waters at the thought of crunchy fried bread and egg-nog. I'm awake. No turning back now.

My tiny feet pat the floor; hands reach for the rough wall. Dust embeds into my fingerprints. There is a stumbling towards the light. Hungry. Like a rabbit staring into oncoming lights. A careful staggering because I want to surprise Nana and I'm half awake. Further and further up the passage, closer and closer to the light. Push back the curtain and I am born into the kitchen. There is Nana sitting at the laminated kitchen table. The same table I was washed on as a baby. The same table on which she serves birthday cakes, baked dinners, cheese on toast. No silver service. Nana eyes me over her glasses. She is already having her third cup of tea for the day.

This is my first memory of Nana. This is my first memory of Coober Pedy.

But I've already forgotten what she said, the words she used. There is just her image, the static of the radio and the heavy smells of breakfast. It makes me sad to realise this memory is incomplete.

Memories fade, like a drought of the mind . . .

I had thought Nana had been formed ready-made from the dust and had forever lived in the hole in the ground. The dugout itself formed her in its womb and the wind blew life into her, and the occasional rain that makes the wildflowers bloom added moisture, added form. She emerged born, from a small opening in the ground, pushed into the dust and the heat and the desert of an opal-mining town.

To say Nana was beautiful would be a blatant exercise in bias, but I am swayed by love and memories, so indulge me.

Nana had an intelligent, kind face. Dark brown pebbles for eyes that either stared at you myopically behind glasses or shined with laughter. She carried the high cheekbones and prominent forehead of her family. Her lips thinned into a lopsided smile. Her skin a pale caramel that faded with age.

Her long grey hair was pulled back and anchored by an enormous bun. Later she would get sick of yanking the brush through it when it hung to her waist. Arms aching. She had it cropped short and cool around the ears. Very masculine. Almost severe. Though Nana could never look like a man because her limbs were soft and round after bearing seven children. Her arms were strong and thick with flesh. Her fingers long and beginning to gnarl, like branches of a tree. I thought she could not bruise.

Bruno was all part of the jigsaw. I didn't have to ask why he was there and Nana didn't have to explain. Why? Because he just was. Always. A solid presence in her life, set rough like a muscular, dusty Buddha in the middle of her kitchen. Bruno's accent was a heavy, strong Italian and it flavoured his English like thick coffee. It took me years to work out what he was saying. He smoked Camel cigarettes and drank flagons of pungent purple plonk. He made Nana laugh often and call him a 'bloody bastard' sometimes. He instituted the family obsession with pasta. Nana could cook like any dyed-in-the-wool Italian mama this side of Rome.

As far as I was concerned Nana could do anything. She was indestructible and she came into existence every day with a blink blink of my eyes. Into the kitchen, new, alive, fresh, but always my Nana.

That is possessive, I know, but it never occurred to me that she belonged to all my other relatives, my two younger sisters, my many cousins, aunties, uncles. I thought that Nana would not have been even remotely interested in anybody else, except maybe her next-door neighbour Clara. Maybe she said the occasional civil hello to the workers down at the Lucases supermarket, but what of it?

Nana was there for me, and when I felt benevolent my sisters could see her and love her, but only on a share basis. It came as quite a shock to me that others could have a closer bond with Nana simply by being her children. My mother and her siblings just made up the scenery of my life, like the way trees make up a forest.

Nana

My Nana was a no-frills Nana.

She'd say, 'Pig's arse', 'Pigs might fly' and 'It's up to you, Fub. You do whatever you want'.

She'd say, 'Yeah well.' She'd laugh, even about rude things. On the other hand, me and Mum never really got on very well. I could never cope with her calling a spade a 'fucking shovel'.

So Nana was always there for me. I would stay over in her dugout the best part of a week. Sleepovers, sanctuaries, company and the like. Bruno would go to bed and it would be just me and Nana. Talking about everything and nothing. Then Nana would say, 'Time for bed, Fub.' So I'd go to bed.

When I got older it would be Nana who'd fall asleep in her chair.

And I'd say 'Go to bed, Nana.' I used to sleep next to her; Bruno would sleep in his own room. And I'd say in my sleep, 'Stop snoring, Nana.' And she'd roll over and stop snoring . . . at least for a little while.

Nana used to make breakfast with thick slices of continental bread. Frothy eggnogs with a whisk in a dented saucepan. The first time Nana used a blender we left the lid off to see how it would work. Eggnog splashed up onto our faces and dripped off the ceiling. We laughed but I'm not sure how long it was before she used the blender again.

Pork chops with apple sauce and wonderfully soft mashed potatoes. Pumpkin scones. Chicken soup when we were sick. Oxtail or kangaroo tail soup. Any soup with bones in it.

Self-saucing puddings, especially on Christmas Day, dripping with golden syrup.

Toasty toasties. Hot Milo for supper.

Lasagne, gnocchi and spaghetti that would make you forget you were vegetarian. She'd spread the margarine thick and make sure there was plenty of rain water in the fridge.

We'd watch Australia thrash England on the ABC, broadcasted 'direct' to South Australia, via Queensland.

A gallery of art and photos of us all at different ages studded the kitchen walls. A young woman in her deb gown. School photos. Clumsy art from school tacked onto every clear surface around her. Anything was put up to stem the crumbling of the walls, to stop the dust from falling on the couch or into our hair or wafting around the dugout. Dust-covered knick-knacks and pieces of blood-red jasper added to the collection.

The kids drew pictures on the dugout walls, in chalk and ochre. How many kids are allowed to do that these days? How many kids even draw on the footpath outside their houses with chalk these days? I remember draping 'Welcome home Nana' banners on the walls to greet her returns from visiting relatives across the country. I felt she always came home for me, to the coolness of the dugout. To the soft powdery light under the earth. Coober Pedy.

Coober Pedy

Coober Pedy. Red, orange, hot hues of ochre. The insidious dust. The continuous heat. The dugouts deep in the earth, capped by corrugated sheets, some rusted, most banging against each other in the dust-infested wind. No streetlights, no bitumen. A hell hole, a bombsite, an ecological disaster. Like a giant hand scraping up the dirt from the desert floor, ripping open and exposing an ant colony. Only the ants are pink and fleshy and they tunnel for veins of colour in the earth. White man's honey dreaming. They crave the sweet success to wash the dust from their mouths. They leave shells of civilisation on the surface of the earth, like stripped carcasses. Car bodies, smashed-up trucks, empty fibro shacks, encrusted with dust and oil and baked in the sun. In the heat of summer it looks as though life itself is abandoned. The only signs betraying this are the pipes of air sprouting like snorkels from the tops of rocky hills. Or an old car crawling along the main street, its driver half dead from the heat.

Coober Pedy is not a town of romance, or espionage, or murders as many journalists shrill in order to sell newspapers. It is a place you have to live in to understand. And you can't really leave. There are those that never do.

Locals

Locals are people identified by others living in Coober Pedy. A local never identifies himself as one. That would be pompous, big-headed. A local is someone who has lived in Coober Pedy for many years. A local is someone who has had a least one relationship with another local. A local is someone who has been transferred to Coober Pedy under duress and tries to make the best of it. Usually a teacher, bankie, public servant. A local is a teacher born and bred in England who falls in love and has six kids to a stockman. A local is a priest—Anglican, Catholic, whatever—who defies the Church when told to move on. But locals are the ones that claim they can't stand 'this stinking hole of a place' and say they will leave with a grand flourish and have vengeance upon the rest of the poor sods left in their dugouts and dust. If they find opal. Even those who leave always find one excuse or another to return. Sooner or later.

But I can no longer claim that I know the place of my childhood. I could never be a local. Coober Pedy changes with each year that I am away, and you can never go back in time, or place. Even if I hate Coober Pedy. Even if I love it.

Travelling

Before we actually lived in Coober Pedy, before Mum and Dad decided to break away from each other, we used to live in Adelaide and travel to Coober Pedy to see Nana and Bruno for our school holidays.

From our birth my mum was to bring her children to her mum. Like a peace offering.

Mum tells me about when Dad saw us off at the bus station. His wife and first born were on their way to centre of the country. He was on his way to freedom and fun times.

Mum says Dad was wearing a new crisp white shirt, wide collars starched to perfection, black hair slicked back. The only thing tighter than his cream flares was his aftershave. He waved to his woman and baby girl in a cloud of testosterone.

Mum stood holding me, gritting her teeth in anticipation of the long hot sticky ride ahead. She could already feel the dust on her skin, in her hair. Scowling, Mum thrust me into his arms.

'Kiss your dad ta ta, Fub.'

I pissed all over him. Warm, smelly, yellow wee. Down his shirt and onto his flares.

He squealed in outrage. Mum held back fits of giggles.

Cats and dogs often piss in the presence of strong perfume. It is presumed they are marking out their territory in the face of opposition. It must have been the aftershave.

It ruined his evening. It made Mum's. We got on the bus and she waved, smiling with the sweetness of victory.

Dad laughs about it now. What else can he do?

We used to travel with Stateliner. Smelly grimy buses packed with grey filthy seats. Brace yourself, we're about to pass Port Augusta. Set those teeth firm in your gums because here comes the dirt road and the shaking is not going to stop for another nine hours. No airconditioning, no fresh air. Open those windows, let the hot wind rip in and whip around your hair; the dust will stick to your skin, setting the river of sweat to mud. No in-bus videos. You were lucky if the radio worked. Then it was one Slim Dusty hour after the other . . .

Kingoonya

We stopped at Kingoonya. Kingoonya stank.

Kingoonya had a front bar (no saloon) with rude cartoons adorning its walls. A distinctive one showed the male figure as a bolt and the female as nut, with stupid grins on their faces. Someone had thought it was funny. I also remember 'Safety advice in the event of a nuclear attack: crouch down, put your head between your legs and kiss your ass goodbye.' But have a beer first.

Kingoonya also had a toilet and a petrol bowser. Or was it diesel? Kingoonya was always hot. It never rained and if it did it only created mud. The last stop before Coober Pedy. Toilet stop. Concrete structure. Corrugated-iron roof. Was there a roof? I'm not sure now, thinking about it. The toilets were always disgusting. Blowfly infested. You either 'went' or you 'held on' for another four hours. It's a bit hard to hold on when your bladder is being ricocheted around a bus. You could rupture. So we 'went', Mum, Sandra and I. We always did. Everybody always 'went'. Except the men. They went to the bar. Beer really was the only way to cope with a bus trip like this. If they sculled enough they might stay drunk until Coober Pedy.

I never realised that men actually had to go to the toilet like women until I was about fifteen. I always thought solitude, standing between a clump of bushes and gazing off into the distance, hands presumably in the pockets, was generally a male kind of thing. I didn't realise they were pissing. I thought they were just being men. It was a blokey thing. Wasn't it?

So the women went to the toilet. Always waiting patiently. Always polite. Always busting. Mum with her two small girls would be last. It was almost a tradition. I think because she was worried about us being so slow, clumsy and lethargic from the bus journey, the heat.

So we were last. And we took our time.

We came out once to dust settling on the road. There was no bus. There wasn't a soul in sight. Even the bar was closed. There was only a quiet that filled the ears with heat. In the distance the crows mocked us with their 'ark, arks'. We were deserted. We were abandoned. The bus had forgotten us. More importantly, the bloody bus driver had forgotten us! We were too hot, too stunned to panic.

'What are we gonna do, Mum?'

'Wait.'

We waited. We didn't sit down. We just stood there in the sun, the red dust sticking in the corner of our eyes. Diesel lined our nostrils. Grotesque. There was nowhere to sit.

Then from out of a red cloud the bus thundered and groaned under its own weight towards us, churning up its tracks and opening its door to us. Someone had noticed our absence and mentioned it to the bus driver. He was gruffly apologetic.

It was the first time my sister Sandra and I were stranded on the road to Coober Pedy. It was not the last.

Silver

There was the time Dad decided to try out his new silver LTD. A sleek low-slung piece of movable upholstery completely out of place in the desert. He fussed and fretted when we stepped into the car. He didn't want the plush maroon-velvet seats ruined by his grotty kids. Dad coaxed his new 'silver baby' to tiptoe through the ruts that made the Coober Pedy road map. But once he hit the bitumen Dad flattened it. Testing the speed limits against the power of his new engine. Sandra and I slept in the back. Oblivious. The engine hummed and the landscape faded into a deep peaceful grey.

Sickening thud. The tyres surrendered their grip to the gravel.

Soft velvet cushioned the impact as we bounced off the front seats and fell to the floor. Small rocks, splinters of gravel and grit lightly prickled our skin. Pin drops of blood appeared on our hands and knees. We crawled outside to find Dad peeling a red buck out of the crushed radiator.

'Fuck! Fuck! Fuck!' Dad said with each pull on the dead kangaroo's tail.

'You fucking bloody fucking bloody bastard!' Sandra and I stood in front of the remaining headlight. Blood dripped from the animal's mouth. Its head rocked and swung as Dad ripped it from the car. Its big brown eyes still glowed in the headlights. It seemed surreal, lurid.

'What are we gonna do now, Dad?' Sandra asked. I looked around us. No headlights coming in the distance. No tail-lights going back. Just the cooling scrub and the faint mingling of dust. The peaceful black of the night contrasted sharply with Dad.

'I'm gonna screw the fucken thing!' Dad shouted to the night.

'C'mon, Sandra, let's get back into the car,' I said.

But she was looking up at the night sky. At the beautiful silvery Milky Way. The saucepan constellation was so close to us standing on the road. Coober Pedy was so far away. As I looked up, stretching my arms out to the sky, Sandra said, 'Mum's gonna be mad.' We were hours away from anywhere. Dad's beautiful car was a write-off. Dad was still trying to pull the roo away from the chrome bumper. Its legs were embedded in the grille of the car and the steaming radiator gave off a smell of cooking meat. Sandra walked over to touch the dead animal. 'Fab, it's warm and fluffy. Come feel.' But Dad said, 'Girls, get out of the light.' Then quietly, 'Get back in the car.'

'Wonder what Mum and Nana are doing now . . .' I looked to the night sky. The whole world shimmering in a beautiful soft silver white. 'Are you stars looking at us right now?' I whispered to the night.

'What are we going to do now?' Sandra asked again. As we sat on the velvet seats Dad dragged the dead kangaroo over to the side of road. With each laboured step he swore and raged, then pushed the carcass out of the light into the scrub. 'You fucken deserve it you fucken cunt!' He kicked the shadows. Sandra and I weren't shocked by Dad's language. Dad talked like this all the time. When Dad was happy his favourite turn of phrase was, 'Well fuck me dead.'

'Dad's got roo blood on his new trackies,' Sandra said.

Dad had a thing for nylon tracksuits. He would buy the latest brand in bold colours and matching sneakers. He liked to pretend he was a famous athlete. A world-class track and field star. He would go up to a complete stranger and say, 'Look.' He'd hold the collar of his latest tracksuit up to the stranger's face and say, 'See. Manchester United.' Or 'Look, just like Deek.' He never exercised. It was what he called leisure wear. We watched Dad dance with anger in the headlights. The kangaroo's blood drying to a maroon crust on his bright blue Adidas suit.

'Yeah,' I said. We waited for him to calm down.

'Least he won't notice it on the car seats,' Sandra said. I looked at her and we cracked up laughing. Delirious from concussion we couldn't stop. We doubled up on the back seat of Dad's shiny new LTD and laughed and laughed until Dad got back in the car and slammed his door shut. Then we all sat up tense, waiting while Dad swore at his new baby to start.

A couple of dull clicks and nothing. 'C'mon! C'mon! You goddamn fucking cunt!' Dad said.

Sandra and I said nothing. He tried again.

I don't know how or why but the engine sputtered back into life. The soft whirring of the new engine replaced by a distressing squeal. Dad rested his head on the leather-covered steering wheel. But the car was going.

'From a hundred and forty clicks to twenty-five ks an hour. If this is how we're going to get there, girls, well then so be it.' Over us the beautiful night sky shimmered its silver stars upon Dad's baby. We limped along the road until sunrise. Then the heat drew out the remaining water from the radiator and finally killed the car. We still didn't know where we were. Dad pushed the car onto the verge and told us that we would have to hitch.

We sat in the shade while Dad sat on the bitumen in the full glare of the sun. He wanted to make sure no one would miss us and drive past.

After a while we walked over to his spot. 'Dad, it's too hot.'

'It's not that bad,' he said. 'If I give you five bucks, will you go back and sit in the car?' Not that there was anything to spend it on but I said, 'Yeah, okay.'

'But you have to give it to us now,' said Sandra.

'Alright.' Dad got up to take the wallet out of his tracksuit pocket. 'Fucken hell!' he yelled.

'What's wrong now?'

'I can't bloody move!' he screamed at us. 'I'm stuck to the fucken road!' Sandra and I stood there with bare feet. We knew that once the skin of the sole seals with the first step it hardens. The bitumen we were standing on had melted and fused with Dad's blue track-suit pants.

'Here, help me up.' Sandra and I yanked Dad's arms and pulled. A soft tearing sound and we looked down at where Dad had sat. A blue nylon fuzz outlined Dad's seat. We looked at Dad's tracksuit pants.

All that was left of Dad's underside was a semi-transparent plastic weave.

'Jesus Fucking Christ.' Dad walked wearily back to the LTD. Sandra and I followed him to the shade, too hot and tired to laugh.

We sat in the shade of the car until sunset when a couple of pensioners pulling a caravan came ambling up the road. Dad ran up to them holding out his money.

'I'll give you two hundred dollars for a lift,' he begged. The pensioners watched us walking up behind Dad. The airconditioning wafting from their windows smelt of freshly cut cucumber. The woman had soft cool grey curls, and pale make-up powdered her face. She gave us a smile.

'Don't worry about the money, mate. Get you and the girls in,' said the driver. We climbed in the back of their soft cool car. We pulled away from Dad's beautiful shiny LTD. The soft maroon velvet looked sombre and exposed in the glare of the sun. Like the underbelly of a gutted animal. Like a kangaroo split open by a car and left to be flyblown then desiccate on the side of the road.

The pensioners started to amble along once again. Stuck between us on the back seat, Dad lurched forward and offered his cigarettes to the driver.

'Smoke?'

'Sorry, mate, not in the car. Missus is asthmatic.' The soft pale woman turned around and smiled. She reminded me nothing of my Nana. I smiled back though. Too tired. The caravan gently swayed behind us and rocked the car in an affectionate way.

Dad fidgeted beside me. He leaned over again.

'How fast does she go, mate?'

The driver chuckled. 'Sorry if you're in a hurry, but with the van on the back sixty is about the limit.'

Awkward silence.

'Hope you don't mind.'

'Don't mind at all. Thanks, mate.' With that Dad dug his fingers into my arm and hung on all the way home.

$\mathcal{D}awn$

When we took the bus from Adelaide with Mum we would arrive at Coober Pedy in the early hours of the night. The lunar landscape would glow blue. People would step off the bus and mutter to themselves, 'What the hell am I doing here?' It would always amuse us because we knew why we were in Coober Pedy. I think it is why our family doesn't like to travel. To see family is one thing. But to travel for the sake of it, just to look at scenery, that would be different. Then we'd have to ask ourselves the same question.

We would arrive layered with baggage, just before the easing of the dawn. The town would wait in an expectant silence for the first touch of light, the first glow of pale pink, slowly turning viciously into the scorching orange-white of day.

But we were there before that, so we could scurry like mice to the hole in the side of the hill before everybody was awake. Even before the neighbourhood dogs could bark, before the dust would stir under the movement of feet and tyres.

There would be a quiet sneaking, a hushing of

voices, the fatigue of the bus evaporating in the shiver of night air. Our eyes would be wide like possums, sneaking the luggage out of the car. Can you slam a door quietly? It was all pretence because we knew Nana would be awake, listening, in the kitchen at the bottom of the ramp. Waiting. Feet and body pointed towards the front door.

Before we had stepped through the threshold, there she would be. She would virtually fly from the kitchen, ten metres up the ramp, to the front door. A flurry of arms and legs, and a keening of happiness as loud and long as the ramp. Breaking the stillness of the morning.

Mum, Sandra and me, standing there slightly dizzy from Nana's happiness, smiling shyly, sometimes crying with her. As we got older Sandra stopped crying and my weeping only became more melodramatic.

By this time Bruno would have taken the bags and suitcases down the ramp, safe into the womb-room of the dugout. An almost silent hulk of a man. Granite-like in his stature, his muscles. He would be momentarily forgotten in the flurry of female emotion. Like chickens flapping around one another. The feathers wafted around the air.

Mum, when did we move to Coober Pedy? How old was I? The visits and the staying have begun to blur into one. A continuous panorama of events, characters, images and emotions. Was I nine? six? ten?

Knickers on our Heads

It was a time for running around with knickers on our heads. Sandra and I would do things like fall out of windows, draw chalk pictures on the ground, hurl ourselves off pushbikes.

We wore knickers on our bums and knickers on our heads. And not much else. Running around at the top of Nana's dugout, where the floors were dust and the walls were wafers of concrete. Bruno had built this dugout as an expression of love for Nana. He had poured the concrete between the chipboards himself. You could see through the boltholes. Bullets shooting white light into the rooms. Over the top a corrugated-iron roof completed the oven. Down below, in the underground kitchen, the adults huddled over their cups of tea, trying to keep cool.

Temperature

A major difference between adults and children is the ability to ignore extremes of temperature. Children will be absolutely bewildered when their parents scream at them in the middle of winter for playing outside in the sprinkler, without shoes on, when it's around ten degrees. With chilblained feet, goose-pimpled arms and blue lips children ask, 'Why?'

When it was hot we were told not to run around. We would want to play on the trampoline when it was thirty-eight degrees in the shade. Our feet would scorch and tingle with each touch of the tarp. The compromise was that we could play in the top part of Nana's dugout, which was hotter than the blaze outside. The sun belting down on the parched land. The wind whipping the dust into a frenzy. Flinging it hot and stinging against the concrete walls.

The land crept inside and the walls were just thin shells. In the meantime we thought we were safe and ran crazily from room to room, the pale dust clinging to our feet like powder. Playing hide 'n' seek with our cousins. Or just us sisters. Drawing on the grey walls with pieces of chalk or soft pieces of rock chipped from the dugout wall.

Bucket Shower

A concrete bunker with a suspended metal bucket and drain was Nana's bathroom. To work it involved boiling the kettle in the kitchen and lugging it up the ramp, lowering the shower bucket and pouring the water in. The bucket was then hauled above your head and loosely hooked onto the wall. You had to turn the tap at the bottom of the bucket to make the water flow in a fluttering of drips through the shower head.

A quick splash to wet everything. Turn the tap off. Soap up before the water evaporated on your skin. Tap on. Rinse. Once the water ran out, that was it. The fastest shower in history. Nana did this every day for twenty-three years. Old soap is still on the windowsill encrusted with red dust.

Decadence is a hot bath.

$\mathcal{L}$ong-drop

Next to the bathroom, in another concrete bunker, was the long-drop. A site of potential terror and relief. The plastic toilet seat balanced on a shell of concrete above a sixty-foot shaft. Privacy wasn't an issue in Nana's dugout—everybody knew when the toilet was occupied. The spectacular sound effects were discreetly ignored. It didn't exactly cause an echo but the hollow sounds conjured images of being buried alive. We were told to be very careful with Nana's long-drop. No one under five was allowed in there alone. There was a lock on both sides of the door. You couldn't see the bottom. Our cousin Christopher used to like trying to watch the toilet paper float down after he had wiped his bum. We were told anyone unlucky enough to fall down would be dead before they hit the bottom. Methane. You weren't allowed to disturb Nana while she was on the long-drop.

Sandra and I had taken our knickers off our heads

and were standing under the bucket shower. Water was rationed. Giggling and half crazy from the heat, we pushed each other across the soapy bathroom floor, competing for the trickle of water. The bucket threatening to fall and split our heads. We pushed it back and forth. It swung wildly. The water splashed on the walls, evaporating immediately. It was six o'clock. Time for bed for us kids. The sun was yet to set for another three hours. Shivering with energy and still half covered with soap, we dried ourselves.

Sandra started it.

'Let's play a joke on Mum and Nana.'

'What? How?'

'I'll hide in here. You run down and tell them I've fallen down the long-drop.' Her eyes gleamed. She grinned so wide her ears wriggled.

'Oh . . . I don't know. They might get a bit upset . . .' I said doubtfully. Although I was the eldest and the biggest, Sandra was always the most cunning. Fighting, she would plead that she was busting to go to the toilet whenever I sat on her. She'd scream for me to let her go. Every time I would believe it. I still would if she said it today.

'No, they won't. Go on, Fub. It will be funny.' The absolute confidence in her voice overpowered me. Her smile invited inclusion into her world. Absolute acceptance. I will do anything to make my little sister smile.

'Oh . . . alright, but only if you come out straight

after I say it,' I said reluctantly, then I rapidly swung into the potential hilarity of the joke. We grinned at each other like maniacs, our hair dripping in our eyes. Half-crazed and naked I ran down the ramp and yelled, 'Hey, Sandra's fallen down the long-drop!' and waited for their laughter . . .

I have never seen my family move so fast. One second they were sitting around the table sedately drinking cups of tea. The next they moved as a wave and I was assaulted by screaming, keening women. Bruno came up the rear. They were halfway up the ramp before I realised what we had done.

I tried to explain it was a joke. At the top of the ramp Sandra ran out of the bathroom and yelled, 'Surprise!'

The shrieking pitched higher. Sandra and I were slapped and sent to bed. Dragged down the ramp by our ears. Faces and bums stinging. Red.

It was only upon reflection, lying in the dark in Nana's bedroom, that I realised that the long-drop was not a funny place. I knew we had done something wrong because Nana *never* smacked us. I still didn't really know why. How could a nine-year-old really know about death? I was confused. I was ashamed. I knew Nanas were not supposed to move that fast. I whispered into the darkness, 'Sandra?'

No answer. Maybe she was asleep. How could she possibly be asleep after what we had done? I stared into the darkness.

Maybe she had snuck out and was saying she was sorry. I leaned over to see if she was still there. Yep. She was still there. No, she hadn't gone to say sorry. Wow.

Troubled and chaste in my nightie I pattered towards the light that was Nana's kitchen. I pushed the curtain aside. I'm not sure whether it was the blinding light or all the adults looking at me, but I blubbered, 'I'm s-s-sorry!' Big sook that I am.

Once again a flurry of arms, like fluffy chicken wings, flapping, hugging me. I sighed under the weight of forgiveness. In minutes I was sitting on Nana's knees, propped up against the kitchen table. It was only then that I noticed the small glasses of bright amber liquid. Each adult had one.

'What's that?' I pointed to a glass. I was cheeky now, the tears still drying.

'That's whisky.'

Liquid fire. I had never seen it on the kitchen table before. There had always been ornate bottles of liquor; some shaped like boots, sent from Bruno's relatives in Italy. They were never opened and collected dust by the TV. Beer was the drink of choice in this dugout. Tea before noon. Rain water for us kids.

'What's it like?'

'Hot.'

'Hot? On your tongue?'

'Yup. We needed to calm down after your little "joke" on us.'

'Sandra told me to do it. Wasn't all my fault . . . I'm sorry.'

'It's okay, love. We had another scare while you were in bed.'

'What happened?'

'Pusslings brought in a king brown.'

'A what?'

'A bloody big snake, Fab.'

'Was it still alive?'

'Yup and pretty pissed off.'

'Did it bite Pusslings?'

'No, but it went to bite us!'

'Where is it?'

'Bruno killed it with a shovel.'

'And all this happened while I was in bed?'

'Yep, love, it happened right here, right on the doormat.'

'Nana nearly had a heart attack.'

'Another one?'

'Not quite.'

'I didn't hear anything though . . .'

'We didn't want to wake you.'

What they meant was they didn't want to attract our attention and have us running around while Bruno was trying to hit a snake with a shovel.

'Where's Pusslings?'

'Sulking behind the fridge.'

'Poor Pusslings, she just wanted to make you happy.'

'Poor bloody Pusslings, my eye!'

By this time everyone was laughing, happy and mellowed by drink.

'Has Sandra come up and said sorry?'

'No . . . she's being stubborn.'

'She started it.'

'And it's time you went to bed. Come on.'

'Nonnight Nana, nonnight Mum. Sandra will say sorry tomorrow . . .'

Sandra was berated for days. Stern lectures about the safety of the long-drop were issued. Threats given. Sandra just grinned, ears wriggling as always, and matched Nana's glare eye for eye.

The king brown lay curled in an old forty-four gallon drum. A metre in length. With a flat head. Sandra and I got off lightly.

Twilight

Coober Pedy wasn't always moments of panic and reacting to kids going crazy with the heat. The town and the desert allowed for moments of peace. A type of peace inaccessible in the city.

Summer twilight. The time between sunset and night made for moments of introspection. Just wondering about the world, alone and comfortable with the heat winding down to the chill of the night.

Before streetlights and bitumen roads the town would glow pale pink. The dust would cause a haze and blur the setting sun into shades of clashing pinks and oranges across the horizon. Any clouds above, bereft of rain, would streak hot pink, reflecting the fire of the desert, then shimmer to deep violet and finally fade into the indigo of the inky night, seeping from the east, never black until midnight.

It was times like this that I would sit atop the dugout, amongst the rocks and prickle bushes, and feel melancholy. Just feeling, not thinking. Too young to put feelings into words. Just liking the colours of the desert. Liking where I thought I belonged . . .

Occasionally a full moon would rise like an enormous gold coin against the velvet indigo of the night. Shimmering resplendent it would reflect the colours of the sunset in a rich way. Like an operatic diva. The woman of the night, calm, dignified, unforgettable. When the moon rose my jaw would drop. The awe never wavering, never getting used to it. And if the setting sun was still raging its colours, an unspoken drama would begin between the two. The sun and the moon competing for audience. Between the two horizons, I never knew which way to look. And all too soon the sun would set, the colours fade and the moon shrink into the night sky. Its gold turning pale and luminous. The diva shrank back and pined for the sun.

Even if I was nurturing a bad mood, or I was angry

and sulking or having a tantrum, 'I hate him, I hate her
. . . I'm never speaking to her ever, ever again . . .', it
would fade with the day. Maybe that was why Nana
would send me outside. A small breeze might wisp up
some dust or come with the cooling night. The sounds
of the town, muted under twilight, would sharpen and
it would be time for kids to go inside.

I would clamber down the hill and go into the
dugout feeling somewhat more philosophical about
life. Thinking, as all kids do, 'What's to eat?'

So this was the beginning of life in many ways.
In the middle of the desert. An enormous family
that branched from the strong, sturdy trunk of Nana.
Only nobody really knew how far it stretched, how it
covered just about half the continent and was fixed
deep into the earth.

Coober Pedy Christmas

Rellies provided light and colour during Christmases
and were expected as much as the presents and roasts.
Roast lamb, roast chicken, roast turkey, roast beef and
occasionally roast rabbit. That way you could take your
pick. There were vegetables as well of course. But they
weren't as important.

There was the Christmas Uncle Mark ate all the
strawberries while us littlies went swimming at the

local pool. Four punnets of bright red fruit encrusted with castor sugar, sliced and chilling in Nana's old fridge. Us kids dreamed about strawberries as we dived and swam. Talked about them as we lay on the concrete, sunning ourselves like sea lions, our skin turning darker under the sun. We came home hot and thirsty. The bowl was empty and Uncle Mark was snoozing his lunch off under the sign 'Heaven'.

That Christmas everybody was there. Aunty Lyn and her kids, Christopher and Karen. The twin uncles in their midtwenties, Peter and Paul, opal mining during summer in their spare time. They bashed around Coober Pedy in an old blue panel van. On the side Uncle Paul had painted 'The Opal Mining Company—Ni' on it. No one knew what 'Ni' meant and Uncle Paul didn't know either. He told people to ask him when he was drunk. He was at his most creative after a few drinks. And his most obscure, even for him.

Paisley shirts, thick fly-away hair, flares and wild ideas to paint Nana's bedroom into a jungle. 'Like when we were kids,' he said.

Uncle Paul started painting our bunk beds with bright green tendrils. They wound thin and insipid up the polished pine legs.

'How are you gonna do a forest in Nana's dugout, Uncle Paul?' I watched him as he painted each with excruciating delicacy.

'Crepe paper,' he said.

'How?'

The vines looked alien and sickly against the mushroom pinks and browns of the dugout walls.

'We'll hang it from the ceiling.'

I looked up at the dusty cracks above me.

'Where would we put the trees?' I asked.

'Over by the cupboard.' He sipped his beer, then dabbed with his paintbrush. Left some foam on his beard.

'But we won't have any room then.'

'Walk around it,' he said.

'But where are you going to *grow* the trees?' I asked. Uncle Paul put down his paintbrush.

'Are you going to finish painting?' I asked.

Uncle Paul picked up his glass. 'A little bit at a time, Fab. A little bit at a time.'

'Yeah, but how?'

Uncle Paul took a sip of his beer and walked up the passageway to Nana's kitchen.

The twins never grew up, their hair just grew longer. No opal. Just incense, wild ideas, loud music, a few beers and a blue panel van that got thrashed and trashed. It's probably been left for dead on an opal field somewhere.

The radio was left on all day, no television for Coober Pedy then, and when the plonk and beer began to flow, the orange plastic record player was cranked up. Engelbert Humperdinck and Tom Jones. Together the family would croon and whine, 'Why, why, why, Delilah?'

Nana's little underground kitchen was packed with fifteen, twenty people one Christmas Day. Sounding like cats brawling at the bottom of a mineshaft.

'The thermometer's reading over a hundred upstairs.'

'Jesus Christ . . . Keep drinking.'

Sweat eased and dripped from each person. Skin felt clammy. Faces shone like wet clay from the heat and the singing. Everybody was trying to keep up with Tom Jones. Occasionally Kamahl was put on to sing a Christmas carol for the kids. Over us all the fan turned in vain.

Nana set fire to the Christmas pudding. It had been collecting dust in its calico bag above the fridge for months. The pungent smell of brandy enticed us to singe our hair on the pudding's flame. Then Nana smothered it with hot custard.

We ate it and spat out the pennies.

'Caaaack, caaaaack.' Christopher choked on tuppence.

'Quick someone, thump him on the back.'

Out it came, spattered in saliva and pudding lumps. Christopher gagged then howled to his mother.

'What'd you try and swallow that for, Chris?' said Aunty Lyn. The old money was put in a pile. Scrubbed and saved to spit out next year.

All us kids were sent upstairs to play. Everyone

became reckless, half mad with the heat. Brothers and uncles began to argue. Others passed out on spare beds. Kids started to grizzle and whinge.

'Mum, I'm bored . . . Mum, Christopher's picking on me . . . Mum, can we go to the pool again?'

Nana surveyed her family in the day's wake. She rallied the grandkids to clean up the mess. The three cordial punch had melted into brown sludge. She poured it down the long-drop. Another Christmas was over with.

'Never again,' she muttered to herself. Knowing full well it was a lie.

With this Christmas I realised that my family existed. It was not just Nana and I. And not just when I opened my eyes. These people existed for everybody all the time across the continent. Uncle Mark from studying down in Adelaide. Uncle Peter and Uncle Paul from wherever they felt like it. Aunty Lyn, Christopher and Karen from Tennant Creek. Other uncles from Arnhem Land. But none from the river country . . . They came to Coober Pedy in pilgrimage to Nana. They each came with their stories. They talked about when they were kids.

Castor Oil and Oranges

They ribbed Nana about her castor oil and oranges.

Castor oil and oranges for constipation. Castor oil and oranges for limp hair, sore throats, sore ears, skinned knees, bruised egos. Castor oil and oranges for everything. Foul, acrid, slimy stuff. It coated the tongue, the back of the throat. The acid from the orange would eat the muck away. It was a fashionable theory at the time—if a child was cranky, or played up, they needed their system cleaning out.

And how they played up . . .

Like the time Nana brought new woollen blankets for the beds. Peter and Paul scraped all the new warm fluff off the blankets and curled it into balls. They left one on each bed for Nana to find.

Nana said, 'They just have to sleep cold this bloody winter. I'm not buying new blankets, that's for sure . . .'

Like the time Jeffrey and Earl lined Peter and Paul up against the back shed to try out their new slug guns. Target practice. Lanky, long-legged kids. Dark skin and dark eyes squinting into the sun as their big brothers lined them up.

'Ouch! That hurt, Earl.' Plink, plink. A couple of slugs strayed off target and hit the tin shed.

'Just you keep still, Paul. It's just a little sting.' Plink, plink. Uncle Earl was the eldest of the seven. Tall, handsome in a rugged fashion, his skin shone dark and healthy. He was the hero of the household. He looked like his father. At the very least he was the boss.

'I don't wanna do this any more, Earl.'

'Just you keep still. It doesn't hurt.' He was old enough for the others to believe everything he said. He wasn't old enough to know better though.

Plink, plink.

'Mum! Earl's shooting at me, Mum!'

'Come back here, ya little runts!' said Earl but his little sibs took off. No more target practice.

Then there was the time my mum Nola took to whacking her brothers with a big stick.

'We used to call you little Hitler, Nola,' remembered Uncle Paul one Christmas past.

'Shut up or I'll thump you right now, ya little shit.'

Poor Uncle Paul. You can never grow out of being the youngest of seven.

He tried to take it out on the kids next door. He thought he would play a trick on them and build a trap in their cubbyhouse. It took him ages to dig the hole and lay branches and leaves over it. He hoped they would fall into it when they returned from their dinner. Only he forgot it was there, and feeling lonely he wandered over, only to fall in the trap himself. Paul never quite fitted in. Childhood photographs show him in sports teams and school groups. Black and white images of him always standing near the margins.

Smirking and out of uniform. At the Christmas concert he tripped over a power socket on stage and blacked out the school.

Aunty Lyn and Nola would snarl and scratch at each other like cats.

See the black and white photos. Their hair is long, sleek and black. Skirts are short to show off their long, dark legs. Here's a photo of them as marching girls. They stand side by side, hands on hips. Twirling batons ready to hit anybody giving them shit. Only their smiles are brighter than their brass buttons. Another photo shows them with enormous beehives. Their eyelids slicked with shiny blue and lurid green.

'Took us a week to get those hairdos down,' says Nola. 'The stuff the hairdresser used was like bloody boot lacquer.'

'Too right,' says Lyn. 'We just had to let it melt down.' They laugh.

'Hey Nola! Do you remember that girl who slept with her false eyelashes and a wig?'

'What was her name again?'

'And when she went home with that bloke he woke up to find a pair of lashes and a wig on the pillow the next day.' They cackle and howl.

'Stupid bitch,' Nola says.

'Oh, she was alright.' Lyn pours another drink.

They claimed licence as sisters to fight and defend each other as they pleased. They called each other every name under the sun. But never a word could be said against them by anyone else. They moved to separate ends of the continent. Lyn followed her heart to Darwin, Nola to Adelaide. They would ring each other, maudlin and melancholy, after their children had gone to bed.

Uncles Earl and Jeffrey went off to be jackeroos. One didn't come back.

Uncle Mark dipped into competitive swimming. His coach said he showed great potential if he could just put on a little bit more weight. Nana worked extra hours to buy him steak.

'I want some steak too, Mum,' the twins would chirp. 'How come Mark gets more than us?'

Out would come the castor oil and oranges.

Uncle Paul said, 'You know, Mum, when you went to the shop, when you came up that hill, if there were oranges in that bag, we just took off.'

Nana would chuckle. 'Well, it worked, didn't it?'

When they were cranky, 'Hey you! You got shit on the liver? Wanna do a goona? I'll get you some castor oil, that'll fix ya.'

What a swag of kids. What a life.

Run kid, run. Don't go whining around no parent when they mention castor oil and oranges.

Corn

When all the uncles and aunties used to talk about their childhood memories I had the feeling they were talking about elsewhere . . . somewhere unknown and mysterious. Their stories seemed mythical, never quite believable because I couldn't imagine a place other than Coober Pedy.

Like the story of flogging corn from the next-door neighbours.

'We used to jump over the fence and move as one towards the patch. When it was just dark, so that old Mr So and So couldn't catch up. Oooo, it was good, that corn, fresh from the stalk, the milk sweet and cool.'

They'd laugh. Their faces aglow around the camp fire. Talking and drinking long into the night. Until the mood turned melancholy and I was sent to bed.

'Go on, get!' Then I would hear old country and western music start up. Pretty soon someone would croon along.

I kept thinking the corn-growing season was just around the corner in Coober Pedy. Long green corn-stalks would miraculously sprout overnight from the parched earth, the talc dust, and we would run across to our next-door neighbours and flog their corn. Perhaps Nana could grow it. She didn't, but I kept looking for it. Where was the corn?

Gone with their childhood, so easily swept aside, like dust. Gone now. These kids of Nana's are no longer children. And the lush green landscape of their youth? Not here with the sun and the wind and the desert.

One bleary morning I stood on the concrete of Nana's dugout. Just looking out over the town, over the land. The stony desert plain stretches from the town to plateaus on the horizon. They are hills worn flat by wind and time. Exposed white talc gives the illusion they are covered in snow, despite the shimmering heat.

'We are dolphins, Fab, don't forget that,' my hungover uncle told me.

I looked at him quizzically, like how children think adults are the dumbest people in the world. Then I looked out from Nana's dugout, over the horizon of desert and thought, 'How can we be dolphins when there isn't a drop of water to be seen? When the only swimming to be had is at the old school pool full of acrid bore water?

'How could we be dolphins in this desert? When this was all I've known?'

3. The Undeclared War

Life is Hard

There was a moment, before realisation, before seeing Nana as she was. It was before university, before I understood the meaning of the word 'history'. I was fifteen, and all that mattered was the 'now' of my life. All that mattered was that Nana was there for me, right then, right there. I had been complaining about my life, about the complications of being a teenager, the small injustices made against me, just whingeing. Once again we were in an uncle's garden, only this time it was down in Adelaide. I was sprawled out on the lawn. Enjoying the sun. Hoping to tan. Nana was sitting on her chair. In the shade. Cup of tea in one hand, cigarette in the other. We were quiet.

I sighed and said, 'Life is hard.' Nana transformed.

Her humour evaporated, drew into her like a mist. Her face hardened. She eyed me and said quietly, 'What would you know of a hard life, hmm? You've never had to scrub floors, to work from sun-up to sunset. You have everything you could want. What would you know, Fab?' Her words and anger faded into a sigh.

I could only respond with surprise. I was wounded because she had never told me of her life before. Now here was a spark of anger, just a glimpse of her hardship. She was right, I had no idea. We let the moment pass.

Learnin'

And so I go through school. I write to Nana in Coober Pedy, telling her everything is alright, telling her everything I might be studying: classics, English, drama, biology. I build an enormous totem pole creature for my art exam. The teachers are worried it could fall and crush other students. I drape it in the ochres and oranges of the desert. I give it black hands, moulded from my own, beseeching. The principal asks if he can have it for firewood after assessment.

I learn to censor my letters to Nana, as any teenager does. I tell her all the good I'm doing. Omit all the bad. I tell her how I'm learning about Pompeii, about what they used to eat in Ancient Rome. I tell how I've learned that Greece has the oldest civilisation in the world, how their culture has been evolving for thousands of years. Nana writes back with love and pride.

Well, dearest, all exams are over for you this year. I was thinking about you all day and hoping it all went your way or most of it anyway . . . When are you coming up? It will be beaut to see you again . . .

Only each year her handwriting scrawls more and more out of shape, words strung together loose and fragile.

This is just a short note, as I want to post it this morning so you can get it as soon as possible . . . I am sending you the money enclosed so you can get the outfit you have on lay-by . . . call it a Valentine's Day present . . .

The paper is becoming thinner, almost translucent.

Sending hankies. I hope you like them, love. They are your Great Nana's. Your Mum said you like hankies. Also the money is your Christmas present . . .

There are moments of melancholy.

Dearest Fab, wishing you all the best ever for a wonderful birthday. I am sending $100. Please get yourself something nice. Have a beaut birthday. Will be thinking of you all

day. Miss you very much, you have been away too long.
Please take care.

But I don't notice them.

Years later I realise it would've taken Nana so long to save all the money she sent me over the years. She was on the pension. No opal came in. One hundred dollars would've taken months of scrimping and saving.

I am too brave; I am too young . . .

These letters I keep in a shoebox under the bed. They move with me from school to university, where I decide to learn about my history, the history of the country I live in.

$\mathcal{D}$ispossessed

I enrol in Aboriginal Studies. I am the youngest. A lone female. My face is the whitest.

Full of enthusiasm I sit at the front. The black men sit at the back. I think, 'So this is what it's like to be in a minority.'

The lecturer leans on his podium. His face is grey.

In many places a grey face means death. If a grey man with grey skin and grey eyes walks towards you, run. It means there is illness or death or pain on the way. So, if you can, turn your face from the shadow and run away. For many Aboriginal people illness and dying makes the blood drain from the skin. Colour does not fade but the brown turns grey.

'You are not here to learn to be good little Aborigines. You are not here to learn where you are from.' He looks at me. 'You will not learn to be Aboriginal here.'

'But I want to know where I am from.' Did I say that out loud?

'We are not here to give you the answers.' The conversation is surreal. 'You don't belong here.'

'So where do I belong?'

'You are dispossessed. You don't belong anywhere.'

'I know where I was born.'

'But that's not where you are from.'

This deeply offends me. How dare he tell me I am dispossessed. How dare he tell me I don't belong. He smiles at me with patronising eyes. Betrayed, I feel small and want to run from this grey man. But there is nothing I can do. I am the mouse played with by the academic cat. Is this what it's like?

After class, a tall man with a face like leather whispers, 'Don't give up. Don't leave. I know what you're thinking. We'll lick that fella yet.'

He smiles. 'We're all dispossessed here, girlie. That's why we all belong.'

He laughs, his voice booming and echoing through the hallowed corridors. Red-faced, I smile.

Lesson

And so, like a 'good little Aborigine' I find all the books in the library and take them home to read. I am slightly bewildered by the titles,

Blood on the Wattle, Frontier, Rivers of Blood, A Secret Country, Contact . . .

Such a preoccupation with blood, I think to myself. What blood? How crazy is this university course? How crazy am I to be here? But like a good little student, a good little Aborigine, I do my homework. I study to pass and I want to learn this lesson in dispossession . . .

I lug the pile home; I snuggle down in my warm safe room, the box of letters under my bed.

Milk

Cold milk and biscuits to sustain my reading, I open the pages to my history.

Was Australia settled or invaded? pioneered or conquered? won by sweat or won by blood? Was it the fruit of industry or a prize of war? These are questions, which have reverberated through Australian history . . .

I'm chewing my biscuit, taking a sip of milk. I read on. These questions may have 'reverberated through history' but they had not reverberated through me before. Perhaps this is a particularly militant book.

I put down one book, pick up another.

William Dampier, the first English navigator and explorer to 'discover' Australia, shot dead an Aborigine as he came ashore . . .

Few are aware that beneath the tranquil face of the North Coast of New South Wales lies a history steeped in blood. Hundreds of the region's Aborigines were killed by European colonists last century. Massacres took place . . .

Many Aborigines fought back, but spears, boomerangs and nulla-nullas were no match for guns and poison . . .

European accounts give this story: Aborigines had been blamed for the theft of flour from the huts of shepherds on Ramornie Station, about 16 km west of Grafton. When George McDonald, the New England Crown Lands Commissioner, visited the area with his Border Police an expedition was formed for 'dispensing justice'. The horse and foot party of squatters, stockmen and Border Police found several hundred Aborigines camped on a bank of the Orara River.

During the night they formed a cordon around the camp and moved in at dawn. The Aborigines were awakened by the crack of musketry, accounts claim. Men, women and children were shot down indiscriminately. Some took to the river and were shot as they swam.

The Orara carried many corpses into the Clarence, past the new white settlement of Grafton . . .

The robberies for which the blacks had been massacred were found to have been committed by 'a scamp of a hut-keeper named Lynch'.

And another.

It may be stated broadly that the advance of settlement has, upon the frontier at least, been marked by a line of blood . . .

Blood?

Poison flour was a common means of dealing with pilferers by inhuman whites in the early days . . . the innocent being made to suffer equally with the guilty, and whole communities being wiped out for the thefts of a few persons. In this way hundreds of erstwhile friendly blacks became lifelong foemen, seeking revenge.

Thomas Coutts established a station of his stockmen and reduced his 5000 strong flock by half . . . Stockmen refused to work at his station so he gave the local clan a bag of flour in payment for harvesting work done on his property. The flour was laced with arsenic.

The unsuspecting Aborigines feasted on damper made with the flour. Twenty-four corpses were found the next morning . . .

The milk in my glass curdles.

Those who had experienced it said so in books and newspapers, letters and speeches, in public statement and private conversations, in every colony and throughout the nineteenth century. Before the settlement at Sydney was a year old, Governor Phillip and his officers were complaining about a 'state of petty warfare'; and 'open war' . . .

War? I'm thinking. Here? In Australia?

In 1826, the missionary LE Threlkeld wrote home to England: 'You will be grieved to hear that war has commenced and still continues against the Aborigines of this land.'

A naval captain visiting the Swan River in 1832 noted in his diary that there was 'really a most awful warfare' in progress; a pioneer West Australian settler declared: 'We are at war with the original owners, we have never known them in any capacity but as enemies.'

Enemies? We are enemies? With whom?

In northern New South Wales in the late 1830s Europeans felt they were 'in an enemy's country'; the whole region was in a 'state of warfare' . . .

The large campfire of the tribe was alight all that night, and at daybreak the whites, with rifles in hand, started to crawl towards the foe. On the way they noticed a few of the blacks preparing the morning meal.

The sudden devastating onslaught, as the whites opened fire at close range. Instantly there were yells, and blacks raced for their lives in all directions. A second volley brought down more of them. In the deserted camp the Europeans found dozens of little piccaninnies.

The whites pursued the fleeing Aborigines . . . They had gone round the head of Evans River, and along the south bank . . . Once within striking distance of the blacks a volley was poured into their ranks. Altogether over 100 darkies were killed on that headland, and for years afterwards the skulls could be picked up on the spot.

How could this have happened in this country? On this land?

Nausea rises within me.

Does Nana know about this, I ask myself. Is this what really happened here?

We are at war with them: they look upon us as enemies— as invaders—as oppressors and persecutors—they resist our invasion. They have never been subdued, therefore they are not rebellious subjects, but an injured nation, defending their own way, their rightful possessions, which have been torn from them by force.

I am ashamed. I have always thought this country so pure, so right, so clean of the blood of wars that stains other nations.

Isn't that why they come here? Immigrants? They come and they bring themselves and pieces of their culture with them, a piece of the land in their souls, they bring with them their food, colour, life. But most of all they bring their memories. And they stay, they say, 'We love this place, we love the air, the light, see the sky, blue, and the peace . . . There is peace here . . .'

No! No! I slam the pages together.

How many blacks died in the 'species of warfare' fought out along the frontiers of settlement? For many reasons this is not an easy question to answer. Colonial governments showed little desire to count the bodies.

I throw my history books across the room. Cry over an undeclared war.

But no one mentions the refugees of the undeclared war. They walk past us like shadows. They sit under the trees, lie in the gutters like prisoners of war. Their skin hangs from their bodies . . . refugees, glaring, unblinking until someone somewhere yells, 'Truce.' A truce no one can quite believe in.

I go home to Coober Pedy. I tell Nana and she only looks at me. But in her eyes there is compassion, sadness and an understanding. During holidays I hide in her dugout then venture south again to continue my study.

Bank

'Yes, hello, can I help you?' The man behind the counter is brisk. Cold. He thinks he's being efficient. He shuffles some papers around him . . .

'Yes, I'd like to organise my allowance to go into my account please.' I hand him the paperwork.

'Okay, if I could just check your ID, thank you.' He looks at the papers.

'You're a tertiary student, are you?' Knowing full well. Why do they ask such inane questions when the paperwork is in front of their face?

'Yes.'

'And you receive a fortnightly allowance from the Department of Employment, Education and Training.'

'Yes, that's my ID number there.'

'Okay . . .' He looks at the papers, then looks at me, then looks at the papers again. 'Just a moment please.

He goes off to a superior. I lean against the bench and take a deep breath.

What could possibly be wrong? I wonder. I'm putting money in their bank, for Christ's sake.

A fatter man, wearing a darker suit, comes over. Brief, obligatory smile.

'Hello, young lady. I've been given to understand that you would like to have your allowance put into your savings account on a fortnightly basis.'

'Yes, that's right.'

'And this account comes direct from the Department of Empl—'

'Yes, that's what I said.'

'And this allowance is called . . . Abstudy?' He looks down at the papers. The original bank officer has crept up behind him and peers over his shoulder.

'Is there a problem with that?'

'Could you explain what Abstudy is, exactly?' The other bank officer nods in agreement.

'Well, it's like Austudy, except it's for Aboriginal students.'

'Like Austudy, you say?'

'Exactly like Austudy.'

'And your name is Fabienne Bayet?'

'Yes.'

'Well that's an interesting name.'

'My father is Belgian.' I sigh, knowing where the conversation is heading.

'And you say that you're Aborig—'

'Look, I can put my allowance in another bank if you like.' Make a grab for the papers. The bank manager holds them.

'No, no, that won't be necessary. Your account shouldn't be a problem at all.'

'Okay.' Look to the clock. Missed my lecture already.

'However, you will incur fees because your allowance is less than three hundred dollars per week. You understand?' He is smirking now.

'Fine.' Fed up.

'Bruce, fix this lady up, will you.' He walks away, leaving the other bank officer to do the work. 'Glad to be of assistance,' he smirks.

I wonder if bastardry is written into his duty statement?

Boxes are good places to keep valuable things. My Nana kept all her treasures in dusty old tea-chests. But for money you need a bank.

I Know Who You Are

I'm sitting around in the grubby student room, sitting, talking.

An older man walks in. It's hard to tell his age. A new student, I think. No. Everybody knows him.

'G'day, Tony, how ya going?' they ask him.

'G'day, g'day,' he says and walks through the room like he owns the place, like he knows it. He's not new.

'This here's Fab. She's a new student here at Task Force,' says someone.

I shrink and say, 'Hello.'

'Hello,' Tony says. 'Where you from?' Studying my face. It is a common question, almost a greeting.

I roll my eyes and take a deep breath, preparing to explain, but he says, 'You're Bundjalung, hey? You're from Northern New South Wales. River country.'

'How did you know that?'

'Oh, it's on your face. It's that wide forehead, those green eyes of yours, girl.' My mouth opens and closes like a fish.

'I'm probably one of your uncles,' he winks. With this statement I'm wary.

'Tell me more,' looking for proof.

'Not now, gotta go.' He makes for the door. 'I'll talk to you about it later.'

'Okay.'

It's a sign.

I stay in the classes, looking for the answers no one will give.

But every time I see Tony I lose my nerve and eventually his face turns grey and he fades away.

Walk On Your Own Land!

It is a beautiful day. The sun is setting and the ducks dodge boats on the lake that is the Torrens. It is festival time in Adelaide. People are milling around. The air is chilly on the skin but they keep each other warm in their smiles, in their happiness. The sounds and messages of the Bangarra Dance Company are uplifting. I've gone from university student to university tutor. I'm happy to be at the festival cause I can afford it. I am with a friend and we are walking along the banks of the river, smiling . . .

We meet a work associate. A strong Aboriginal woman, educated, forthright. She is a hero. We have met her before a number of times, through work, to ask her about politics, about history. She is articulate, angry about the world's injustices, but always willing to share her views.

'Hello, Iris, how are you?'

She pushes her hair from her face. 'I was alright before you whitefellas at the uni sacked me.'

'Sacked you? Who?' This is news to me . . .

'I can't stand you Gubbas taking Nungas' jobs!' Her chin is thrust out, challenging.

'You know I'm not white, Iris.'

'Yeah, but you're not from this country, are you, Fab?' she jeers. 'You're not Kaurna.'

Her rebuke is like a slap.

'I was born here in Adelaide.'

'Go back to your own country, girlie. Go walk on your own land. You're not welcome here.' She pushes past us, strides away.

I am too stunned to speak. I look to my friend. He holds my arm. My guts squeeze.

'Come on . . .' I'm led away. 'She's just angry because she lost her job.'

'Uh huh . . . I didn't know . . .' But the sounds of the festival are muted now and the setting sun chases the warmth.

Annotated History

It is a time in my life when I think I can do the most good working in an institution. It is a time and place in my life were the 'good' becomes weird and Aboriginal people are thin on the ground. They are not to be found behind computers, cocooned within grey shell-like transportables floating above a surreal landscape where the introduced fish are the only things to survive in the urine coloured river.

Giant carp cruise like a group of bikers beneath paddling native ducks. I watch their fins for tattoos reading 'Mum', 'Love' or 'Harley Forever'. The brown ducks nervously waddle up the bank to get out of the water. It seems safer to beg from humans than to fish.

Ducks afraid of fish. A tiny capsule of absurdity set in a grey world of isolation. Small moments and situations can trigger the search for more than just history written on paper.

But that's the world outside. In the sunshine. I'm within the cocoon. A pale grey office setting. Everything is grey and plastic.

Impassive dull carpet, grey laminate surfaces. There is no texture here. The walls are pale grey. Even the window is tinted grey so as not to disturb the delicate disposition of the precious computers. Four of them sit on a grey bench, bolted to the wall at waist height. There are no chairs along the bench.

'Because computers don't sit,' I say to myself. Am I in a dream world? Am I in a nightmare? Am I talking out loud?

'It's okay because there's no one else,' I say again.

I sit at a large grey table in the centre of the room, where no outside light can reach. There are about six chairs around this table. One is wood. I hauled it out of the river a few weeks back. Let it dry out in the sun. The wood has warped and is painful to sit on, but I'm sick of the grey. Sick of it. Wondering how I bloody got here.

Above the computers is a state of the art whiteboard. It runs the entire length of the room. Bolted just out of arm's reach.

I've been given three weeks to write the history of

Australia from an indigenous perspective. A crash course in massacres, blood, legislation, struggles, marches, deaths. It's all so overwhelming.

I'm imagining the computer is my brain encapsulated in grey plastic. I'm projecting images and words onto the whiteboard from my computer-brain.

An image of a snake painted in 'Aboriginal' style swirls into photos from historic documents and drawings of massacres, hangings, battles, Aboriginal missions, Aboriginal people in chains. Words like: NATIVE TITLE, BLOOD, MASSACRE, REFUGEES, FORGOTTEN SOLDIERS, NO ONE WAS HERE, THE ENEMY, SHOOTING PARTY, TREATY? interchange with the image of the snake throughout.

I'm stuck on the 'undeclared war'. I'm supposed to stop at *Mabo*. But history keeps unfolding itself.

'How the fuck am I going to finish this?' I say to the whiteboard, the computers. I wonder if I'm losing my mind. Maybe I've been possessed by the computer.

'Maybe I don't exist at all. Maybe that's why I can't keep up,' I say to the airconditioned grey.

A work colleague opens the vault door. She's a friend of mine, same age, midtwenties. She dresses in an 'arty' way—bright colours, mismatched textures, long curly hair hennaed bright copper. She's hired to design the Dreaming Serpent I'm imagining projected onto the whiteboard. She's not Nunga. We call her Crystal. She does great computer graphics. She's like a rainbow walking into the room and I'm the little black cloud within the grey squall.

'Fub.'

'Crystal.'

'You alright? You look a bit stressed there.'

'Yep.' I sit up. 'Yep. I'm fine. How ya going? How's the Dreaming Serpent going?'

'Not bad. I've nearly finished putting in the era titles you wanted.' She flops an enormous polyester folder onto the table in front of us. With a great sweeping motion she unzips one side and hands me two floppy disks.

'Great,' I say. I look to the computers staring at me along the bench. I can't be stuffed getting off my warped chair.

'So . . . what are you doing?' Crystal asks as she stretches out on the carpet.

I'm looking down at Crystal stretched out on the carpet and I'm thinking to myself, 'My dear, you look like the Dreaming Serpent herself with your rainbow stripes and red flaming hair uncoiled there.' But I don't say it because I'm going mad and I don't know if I'm dreaming myself.

'I'm filling in the history of the Dreaming Serpent. I'm writing about the undeclared war,' I say.

Crystal stretches her arms and yawns, 'Oh, like, you mean the war between the states?'

'The war between the states?' I ask.

'Yeah, like when Western Australia didn't want to join the other states during Federation and wanted to be a separate country by itself.'

'Did it really?'

'Yeah, didn't you know that?' Crystal says, then gets up off the carpet as our supervisor, Bruce, shoulders the door open. He's been jogging and is sweaty and flustered.

It's What You Look Like

'Hey Bruce,' Crystal says but Bruce ignores her.

'Have you finished writing that history of Australia yet?' he asks me.

All I can say is, 'No. Not yet . . .'

'But you've been working on it for a whole two weeks! You better hurry up, because I want to publish it soon.'

'I'll try and get it finished by the end of the week if that's not too inconvenient for you.'

'Good.' He's staring into one of the computers. He's frantically swiping and clicking the mouse. Crystal's Dreaming Serpents come alive across the benchtop. They swirl and shimmer simultaneously to computer-programmed jazz. I'm reminded of electrical stores where rows of televisions are set on the same channel. At least the grey of the room has faded but I've stopped projecting images from my mind. The whiteboard goes blank. Crystal wrinkles her nose at me and smiles.

Bruce turns around, 'Oh, and another thing. You have to stop dressing like a uni student.' With this Crystal gets up from her chair and says to the room, 'I'm just going to go and get some lunch.'

Once the door has sealed shut I ask, 'What d'you mean, a uni student?' I feel as though I'm glued to my chair. The wood has come alive and clenches my buttocks, pinches the folds of my skin.

Bruce points at me. 'Well, if you dress in such provocative clothes no one is going to take you seriously. Not in this academic business!'

I'm feeling dull. I'm feeling trapped. The rainbow of the room has left for lunch. I've got on a white shirt, a black skirt, flat black shoes and my hair has been caught in a bun. It won't be brushed out until I finish the history of Australia.

'So you want me to dress less . . . casually?'

' Yeah, take a leaf out of Noel Pearson's . . . or Marcia Langton's book. Spend some of your money on some . . . professional clothes. It's how you present yourself in this game that counts. It's what you look like.'

Bruce is dressed in a golf shirt and shorts. He is not wearing socks with his running shoes. I'm not projecting serpents or massacres onto the whiteboard any more. I'm projecting four-letter words in bold underlined 72 point fonts just above his head.

'Oh, right. So are you telling me a black woman's gotta dress right?'

But Bruce has already headed for the door, 'Yeah well, better get ready for this reviewer.' And as the door shuts I am sealed back into the nightmare grey.

I've been told to get ready for the reviewer. And maybe I do. Maybe I rip myself from my beloved wooden torture chair and start up another computer. Maybe I sit there and keep staring at the whiteboard. Maybe I walk out of the room, out of the building, out of the institute into the open air. Maybe I breathe. Maybe this whole thing is just a computer-animated dream digitally projected onto an enormous whiteboard. I mean, this is a world where fish scare ducks. And the urine coloured river is banked by concrete. To ease its draining into the sea. Smooth its dying pillow, so to speak.

Maybe. What does it look like to you?

Maybe I take out my bag and open up myself from it. Maybe I undo the strangulated bun and let all that thick long tangled hair fly. In the bag I will find a pair of long black-yellow-red earings. Perhaps I will put these on, take out the pearls, and redraw these pinched lips with a deep ochre red. Perhaps it's the colour of old rust. Maybe it's dried blood from biting my tongue. You choose. Up on the whiteboard I've untucked the blouse from my skirt like I used to at high school. And

I've put my reading glasses on the grey table and used the absolute latest high-tech superexpensive state of the fucking art laptop to smash my eyes into smithereens.

Back in the room Bruce walks in and flips open the intact laptop and plugs it into the other computers.

'Okay,' says Bruce, 'Now, this reviewer is a really strong black woman.'

I respond, 'You make her sound like a cup of coffee.'

There's only a brief pause. We look at each other. Here's an undeclared war.

Bruce continues. 'She doesn't mince her words and she's not impressed by the way the rest of the university has been spending money. She's a real radical, so be nice to her otherwise she'll give us a bad report. Just show her what I've told you, be polite and we'll all be better off.'

The head of the institute and the reviewer enter the room.

The head of the institute works on the other side of the river. To call her Beth would suggest a degree of softness. A deception because she's a sharp dresser and astute academic. A stunning Aboriginal woman with glossy black hair fashionably clipped, and wearing her trademark fire engine red jacket. She reminds me of a beautiful ladybeetle. Her shiny red fingernails glint as she eloquently gives keynote addresses across the nation and world. She's beautiful but her hard shell does not crack under pressure as she flies from conference to conference. She strongly believes that indigenous education is imperative in the struggle for freedom from oppression. She says, 'It's not settlement, Fabienne, it's invasion.' But she says this gently. She's simply stating facts and when she gives these facts so clearly and sensibly I can't help but agree with her. But when I go back and change my own writing, erase the old soft words and replace them with the new, I can't release myself from my anger. The meaning of these words does not change, regardless of what they look like. But grooming is part of Beth's armour and I'm duly intimidated every time I see her and every time she speaks.

Beth introduces Bruce and myself to our reviewer, Joan Peach. 'And this is the senior research officer. He's in charge of all of our computer technology and heads the Native Title CD-ROM project,' she says.

Bruce and the reviewer shake hands.

'How do you do? It's a pleasure to meet you,' says Bruce.

Joan's formidable reputation surrounds her and blurs the soft floral print on her dress. Maybe I'm just too tired for this, I'm thinking, but Beth continues.

'This is our research assistant. She coordinates all of the native title material. She's currently writing a history of black Australia to be published on the CD-ROM. I'll leave these two capable people to show you the progress of the program. Fabienne, would you be so kind as to escort Ms Peach back to my office afterwards?'

'She'd be delighted to,' Bruce answers for me and that's when I know it doesn't matter what I look like, what I say, what I write. I've just got to wake up.

'Well, if you'd just like to take a seat at the main computer, Ms Peach, I will show you the latest in Aboriginal educative materials.' Bruce is warming up.

Joan sits in front of the laptop and folds her hands. 'I must say I'm sceptical about all of this new technology . . . What I want to know is, does it help Aboriginal people in the community?'

There are some things in academic circles one is expected not to say. We say nothing to this and Bruce continues.

'Yes, well, as you see, this project is at the cutting edge of community consultation. It has the latest information on native title, direct from ATSIC, the latest draft of native title legislation and over a thousand press clippings on the subject . . .' Bruce begins the program. Crystal's Dreaming Serpents rise and swirl again.

'Why doesn't that have Nunga music to it?' Joan asks and I sit back into my wooden torture chamber and wonder who's going to answer.

'That's being added later,' Bruce responds and looks to me for assistance, but I can't say anything. I can only answer for the work that I have done. I can't program computers. I'm here to give an indigenous perspective.

'Now, if I can just show you, the opening sequence begins with two Dreaming Serpents . . . one showing the history of the native title debate since the High Court ruling, the other giving a history of Australia since settlement.'

'Invasion,' says Joan.

Hello. I project onto the whiteboard.

'Oh, yes, invasion. Fab, you'll have to change that of course. Silly really. My apologies, Joan.' Bruce is sweating onto the mouse pad.

'And why is the beginning called the Dreaming?' The reviewer turns to me. Her gaze is hot and all I can think of is the phrase 'strong cup of coffee' and I'm trying to explain but Bruce interrupts.

'Because it's the time before white settle—invasion. It shows the history of Aboriginal culture through archaeological discoveries. If you'd just like to take a look at the impressive computer format.'

But Joan ignores Bruce and the impressive computer format. I feel like a grub that has just been scraped out of her safe cocoon and pinned to a display board. A juvenile ugly translucent larvae not allowed to develop into a butterfly, or black and white moth.

'But why did you use the word Dreaming for the title?' Joan insists and I'm searching for the right academic response.

'Because Dreamtime is derogatory as a category . . .
I was told.' I'm fumbling with the politically correct.

'So is the word Dreaming.' Joan's voice is flat, solid.

'Yes, but I didn't want to call it pre-invasion or
prehistory because that would make it seem like
Aboriginal people are Stone Age people.' I'm reciting
from my internal textbook.

Bruce is nervous and losing control of the conversation. He begins again. 'Well, yes, ladies, if you would
just take a look at the impressive graphics, we can skip
over the chronology.'

But Joan ignores him. She won't let me escape. 'You
should've used a local word for the term. You should've
asked some Kaurna elders.'

The grey of the room seems stifling, suffocating. My
boss is watching me. I'm on the verge of losing my job.

'But it's going to be a national publication. I didn't
want to step on anybody's toes,' I say.

Bruce tries vainly to recapture the conversation.
'Joan's right, you know, Fab, cultural appropriateness
and all that . . . You know I did say . . .'

But Joan snaps at me. 'What would you know, you're
just a stupid white woman.' And with that Bruce flings
himself back in his seat, resigned to the brawl. But my
whiteboard has fractured in two, unnoticed behind us,
and the grey cocoon is splitting open.

'No, I'm not. I'm Aboriginal actually.'

Maybe it was a dream, but then I wouldn't remember

the surprise on Joan's face and the way Bruce puts his head in his hands as if in momentary defeat.

Bruce tries again. 'This is all very interesting, but if I can demonstrate.' He's clicking on his beloved laptop and all the other computers scroll up and down through pages and pages of computer text.

Joan visibly changes before me and I'm already growing my wings, forming a solid body.

'Well, why don't you use your own language then, instead of Gubba words.' Joan leans towards me.

'I don't know my language . . . my family doesn't come from here. I don't want to upset anybody.'

'Ask your elders, they will know. It's important you use our language when you're writing the history of our people.'

'My Nana . . . doesn't . . . remember any more.' There's an awkwardness as I unfold.

'Where are you from, girl?' she asks me, but Bruce stands up and forces Joan out of her chair.

'Is that the time?' he says, looking at his nonexistent watch. 'I'm sure you'll be expected for afternoon tea across the river.'

Joan hands me a card. 'I have a few articles on language use that maybe you would like to read. Contact me any time.

'Stay in touch with your people, don't just call yourself Aboriginal.'

I'm left alone in the room again but this time I want

to carve 'It's what you look like in this game that counts' into the back of my wooden chair. My body wants to leave a mark amongst this wash of electric grey.

But I'm already flying out of here. Through the split whiteboard, through the grey wall. I'm going looking. Blood-red lipstick on my wings and all. Maybe I'm flying out of my nightmare.

The names have been changed. So has the institute. The computers are still there.

Even in a world where ducks are afraid of fish. Definitive history does not fit on a computer because history never stops. And one man's history is another woman's lie. Depends on what it looks like.

Class

I try something different. Move away from the research and the writing and have a go at teaching. Jumping off an island into a whirlpool. Already the river tide is sucking me under.

I'm in a classroom, in a Catholic school. It's a prelesson brief by two supervisors. In their office. They sit down.

The senior supervisor begins: 'These kids are teenagers, most of them would be practising Catholics, and they've probably never met an Aboriginal person before. It will be their first lesson on Aboriginal issues.

Your task is to explain to them the concepts of native title and land rights. Okay?'

'Okay . . . Yep, good.' The coordinators glance at each other.

'Also . . . we need you to know that the teacher involved with this class is very . . . nervous about his students meeting an Aboriginal woman.'

'Nervous?'

'He's worried about you being too militant.'

'Militant? Me?'

The older of the two supervisors sighs and leans forward to explain. 'Basically he's not very happy about the situation. He feels he's built a rapport with these kids at a very delicate time of their studies—assessment and all that—so he doesn't feel very comfortable with you invading his space and putting crazy ideas into their heads.'

'Crazy ideas? What crazy ideas?'

No one answers.

'Oh, what, you mean like cutting a bora ring into the carpet?'

'Something like that.' The sarcasm is lost.

'Well, maybe if he met me he would see that I'm not about to do that.'

Another awkward pause.

'He doesn't feel very comfortable with you knowing who he is at the moment.'

This is ridiculous. Look at me, look at who I am.

How am I supposed to go into a classroom on this basis?

'Maybe I'll just get them to paint the room red, yellow and black.'

'But he's happy to leave you to explain the basic concepts . . . the Dreamtime, land rights and dispossession,' says the younger coordinator brightly. As if in consolation.

'How long do I have with them?'

'Forty minutes.'

'And they've never encountered Aboriginal issues before?'

'Well, some of them may have done some stuff in primary school, but most of them wouldn't have, no.'

'Oh.'

'And there'll be another teacher present, assessing your delivery,' says the older coordinator.

'We will let you know how you go,' comforts the other.

'After this, can I be introduced to this teacher I'm apparently . . . intimidating?'

They exchange glances.

'We'll see,' says one of them. No eye contact.

So I find myself standing in front of a class of very sceptical, very bored, very cynical teenagers. It's my first lesson.

First Lesson

It is after lunch. It is hot. The walls are brown brick, the school uniform is dark brown, the carpet is pale brown. The whole atmosphere is dull.

Clutch the duster and chalk. The supervising teacher has not arrived.

The students are wary. They pile their bags on the desks and hide behind them. It is a barrier for them. The eager ones sit at the front. In the last row the boys lean back on their chairs, they hook their toes under their desks. They dare this student teacher to straighten them up. Eyeing me off.

I'm not taking them up on their challenge and make my first mistake.

'Does anybody know anything about land rights?'

No response.

'Does anybody know anything about the Dreamtime?' I turn away from them with relief and write the words, Dreamtime. Land rights.

There is a silence, then only a giggle from one of the girls. First rule of teenagers—don't volunteer anything.

Sweat. Five minutes have passed and the supervising teacher still hasn't arrived.

I've got nothing to lose. I've got thirty-five minutes left.

'Okay.' Throw away the chalk and duster.

'Alright, I've been told that you're all practising Catholics. Yes?' There is some nodding of heads.

'Well, I'm not. So instead of talking about the Dreamtime—that's the word used to describe the Aboriginal belief system—let's just say the Dreamtime is something like the creation of the world—it is creation—and we'll go into the details a bit later on.

'So, right now, I've been told you need to define the words: dispossession, land rights and native title.' The students look at me like I'm crazy. It seems I've totally lost them.

Drive

'Which one of you has a car?' The boys at the back briefly stop talking.

Take a deep breath. 'It's a beautiful car, a souped-up Torana you bought from your cousin after saving for two years. It's got new seats. It's painted metallic blue. You've installed the stereo in it yourself. And more importantly, it's yours. It's not your parents' car. It's not your big sister's. It's yours.'

Still silence, but imagine it's no longer threatening.

'Anyway, you love this car because you live in the middle of nowhere. You got your licence and you can go anywhere you like. You don't need to ask your parents to drive you into town on Saturday night. You can pick up your girlfriend in it. You can do the late shift at Maccas and get double time for it because now you have your own transport. You can go to the footy in it, go and see your friends in it, go for drives with your friends, whatever you like—within reason.'

The boys at the back are nodding. At this point in time I have their attention. A couple of the students in front have moved their bags to the side of their desks.

'You have your freedom, you are finally independent. You are an adult. Everything you have been working towards in your life is in your very own car. Maybe even once you've finished school, you will be able to sell your car and go overseas for a year before going to uni. It's your ticket to freedom. It's your ticket *out*.'

The students are listening, curious. What has this got to do with native title and land rights? See the question on their faces.

'Okay, so imagine what it would be like if you totalled it. Through no fault of your own. A truck goes through a red light and wipes your car out. You're alright, but your car is gone.'

Pause.

'Now, you don't have any insurance. You don't have any savings, because all the money you had went into maintaining your car, and now it's gone. Imagine that.

'You are stuck at home. You have to ask your mum or dad if you can go out, you have to ask for a lift when you can. You have to rely on their money, them feeling generous, but they're not feeling generous at the moment—because they can't trust you any more because they think *you* crashed your car. Your friends can't see you any more, except at school, because none of them have a car and they live too far away. You lose your part-time job because you can't work the late shift any more and they now think you're unreliable, so you don't even have any money to catch a bus. And your girlfriend drops you because her folks think you're a dangerous hoon. Imagine that.'

At this point the mood in the classroom has taken a turn for the worse.

'Through no fault of your own, you've lost your friends, your job, your freedom, your security and your future. And you can't get it back.'

The students are wondering what the point is.

'Now.' Take another deep breath. 'Imagine that your car was your house and your land. And your parents are the government.

'You can't work. You can't go out. You can't see your friends. Can't go to the footy, or shopping, you are branded as a trouble-maker and no one trusts you any more. You had your freedom and independence and now, well now you're treated no better than a little kid. Imagine, through no fault of your own, they took it away. You were minding your own business. You just got in the way of a speeding truck.

'That is dispossession.'

There is a quietness in the room. The cogs in their heads are whirring. At least I hope so. No one is smiling. The boys at the back of the room are looking a bit pissed off.

'Or sort of . . .'

The supervising teacher has just come in. Now is not a good time to lose grip. Continue.

'But you've still got your own bedroom, right? You're still at home with your folks and all. It's okay, isn't it?'

I'm smiling, trying to loosen the students up a bit. And thinking, I haven't even mentioned the massacres, the killings, the disease, how the enemy parties would kill the children first. How some used to play croquet with babies' heads. No, I can't mention any of that . . . Keep talking.

'It's your bedroom, right? You've got your bed in it, you've got your stereo, your desk where you do your homework, your posters up on the wall, clothes on the floor. You've finally managed to kick your brother or sister out to their own room. And now this space is all yours.

'But is it really yours?'

'It's your parents' house, isn't it? They own it, or they rent it. They decide how it's decorated. Who sleeps where.'

If only the absent, frightened teacher could come in

now and see the radical, militant Aborigine that I'm supposed to be. I'm talking interior decorating.

Continue.

'Say your parents decide that they are going to redecorate, so you're kicked out to the lounge room. You have to sleep on the sofa for a month while your parents strip the carpet. All your possessions, except maybe your school uniform and your books, are chucked in the shed.

'One day while you are at school, they take all your posters down and chuck them in the bin. They argue that they didn't like the influence these posters had on you anyway. All your music and your stereo have been packed and put in the shed as well. You're not allowed to play your music on the lounge room stereo. And because you are in the lounge room your parents tell you when you have to get up. They tell you when it's time to go to sleep. You don't have any privacy and your friends don't come over.

'You come home and there is nothing left in your room.

'And then, to add insult to injury, they paint your room lime green or hot pink and orange, then they make you move back in.

'It's not really your room any more, is it?' I ask, not waiting for an answer.

'It never really was in the first place. And your folks have no hesitation in reminding you about that.

'That, in a way, is what land rights is like. Except it's not just a bedroom, or the lounge room, and it's not your nice familiar parents. It's the whole house, it's the whole block where you live, it's the whole suburb. You were moved out whilst it was rearranged, and then you where allowed to move back, but only under certain conditions.'

'That sucks,' says one student at the back.

'Except your parents are the government—they don't know you personally and so they don't really care,' I continue.

By this time the class looks worried. There are so many questions in their eyes and time is running out. Give them something else to think about. Homework.

'So, the policy of land rights could in effect be described as being allowed to live in your bedroom and to call it your bedroom. But without having a choice about what goes in it or what gets taken out of it. You can't decide who visits, and your parents/government can take you out of it at any point in time. It is not secure. It is not ownership. You can say it's your room but it isn't really.'

The supervising teacher is looking out the window with a strange expression on her face. Five minutes to go.

'As for native title—well, let's just take this theme one step further. Native title is like if you had to live in your parents' lounge room permanently, but the name stuck on your bedroom door, well, it can stay there. Everybody in your house, your parents, your brothers or sisters, your Great-Uncle George, still says the bedroom's yours, but you're not allowed in it. And maybe, just maybe, if it's a really important assignment and only if you ask for permission, you're allowed to do your homework in there.

'Native title is very much like that.

'Are there any questions?' No one says anything. Did I completely bugger it up?

Pick up the chalk and duster. Keep talking.

'I can see that this is somewhat confusing for you. And we'll talk about the reason why next lesson. I have not really given you definitions of these terms as such, but what I've tried to do is . . .'

But with that the lesson bell rings and the class automatically rises from their seats, rushes out, like a herd of stampeding cattle, on to their next class, on to something else . . .

Yell out over their heads. 'What I'd like you to do is to write down how you might feel if these things happened to you and . . .' But they are all out of the room before I've finished my sentence.

So much for chalk and talk.

I'm no good at this teaching game.

Maybe there is something else I could do . . . But life stops, briefly, and takes a new turn.

4. Lookin' for Ullagundahi Island

Fractals in the Landscape

My Nana has a stroke. Simple as that.

She was just bending down to pick up a packet of cigarettes.

At the top of the ramp.

In her dugout.

Nothing sophisticated in that.

Then she fell.

But she couldn't get up.

So now I'm flying up there, the plane droning, ringing in my ears, making me nauseous. The sun glares through the small windows, hurting my eyes. The airconditioning somehow defies the sun beating its heat into this metal plane. I have to crane my neck to look outside, to see the clouds, to see the land below. My body is confused, suspended so far above the earth, cramping from the cold air around me, blinded by the sun coming through the windows. The air hostess, comfortable in this totally unnatural state, offers me reconstituted orange juice and dried cake. I'm physically suspended five thousand metres above the earth, every pore on my skin is screaming to be down, to be on the solid ground, and she wants me to eat.

I want to be home, by the sea, or safe in my mother's dugout at Coober Pedy, even enduring the twelve-hour bus trip on the Stuart Highway. I do not want to be up here. I try to concentrate on the landscape below, on its patterns, on how the sun and dust feel on my skin when I'm way below, down on the ground, walking the earth, like I'm supposed to.

From up here it is a marbled landscape. Fractals in hues of browns, rose browns, mushroom pinks, red the colour of dried blood, swirling, splitting into thousands of branches. These are the rivers of the Pleistocene. All dried up now, but their patterns still remain.

The trees that line the riverbeds, almost in perpetual hope, look black from up here. Their deep dark green is an indication that somewhere, deep below, there is cool water seeping through the rocks, through the black. Maybe the trees suck this darkness from below into their leaves. They know where the water is. They know its dark and cool. Pale men venture out here, into what they call 'the middle of nowhere'. Forty-degree heat is not uncommon. The stones shatter into thousands of pieces because of the ice-like nights. But pale men think they are stronger than stones and smarter than trees and they come out here with their arrogant ways. They think they don't need the darkness of the trees. They won't follow the patterns. They ignore the laws of this landscape and think a change of government will change the land.

But the landscape teaches the men, it whispers to them, as soft and incessant as the wind. 'You must become part of me, one way or the other. You must take on my features, you must take in the brown, the dust. You must learn from the stones and the trees or you become dust.' This is what the patterns whisper to me. These men, they become weathered. Their faces take on the patterns of the landscape. They learn or they die.

I lean back into my cold seat. I can't cramp my neck any more. The air hostess asks if I'd like another magazine. I refuse. She notices how ill I am. She suggests a Panadol or Dispirin. I shake my head. She leaves me alone. I think about why I am here.

I know all about distance. I've lived either up or down the Stuart Highway ever since I was two months old. My Nana has lived in Coober Pedy ever since I've known her. Now, nine hundred and sixty-three kilometres may not seem like such a distance to those who have relatives across the world, but the distance between a coastal city and a dusty mining town is not so much in the miles but in the mind.

People who visit Coober Pedy say it's like the other side of the moon. Not everybody gets to go to the moon, so I wonder where that analogy comes from. It was my home for six years so it was the centre of my universe. Suburbia and the cityscape are my alienation, my moonscape. There is nothing quite as familiar as a flat horizon, the smell and feel of dust and the sun glaring down on my face.

They said one side of her body was paralysed.

When Bruno found her.

I don't know which side.

But I'd never heard my Nana sound like that on the phone before.

I had to see for myself.

The last time I left Coober Pedy she said to me, 'I know I won't be seeing you for a long time.'

She was tired. Still is.

When I walk into the hospital, into her room, she looks so tired her eyes don't even recognise me. She sits in her bed. There is no glimmer of light, no cry of delight. Perhaps a shy smile.

She doesn't even recognise me.

But I can't falter for a moment. Can't risk a missed beat. I swallow a sob and say, 'G'day, Nana, how's it going?' And hide my face with a hug.

Because it's my turn to be an adult. Now it's my

turn. But there's nothing else to be done in Coober Pedy. It's just going to take time. We visit and sit with Nana, spending her time. I look down the softly lit hospital corridor and remember wheelchair races when I was a schoolkid. A happy, crazy time from so long ago. It seems as though it never happened.

We go back to Mum's dugout to rest.

Standing in the kitchen, peeling spuds, Mum looks calm, determined to get on with the routine of life. I am angry. Confused at the injustice of it all. I ask, 'Why?'

My mother replies, 'Why what, Fabienne?'

We are tentative, impatient and bluffing in our uncertainty, the buffer zone of my Nana has disappeared. Both vulnerable and hurting in our shock, there is no one to translate between us any more.

'Why are you going to look after Nana? How can you look after her? You've got so many other things to do, to get on with your life.'

'Well, who else is there to look after her, Fabienne?'

'I don't know, Uncle Mark said he would. He said that she could come down to Port Augusta.'

'She won't want to leave Coober Pedy, you know that as well as I do.'

'But she can't stay here in Coober Pedy, she can't stay in her dugout. There's no running water, let alone hot water. The ramp is too steep for her.'

'She might want to. Her dugout is her home. Uncle

Mark has said he'll pay for a hot water service. If she gets well enough to go home.'

'Okay,' I say, grasping, wanting to help. 'I'll pay half.'

'We'll go thirds,' says my mum. Not looking up from the vegetables.

'Okay.'

'You, me and Uncle Mark.'

'Okay.'

There is a silence. We continue peeling potatoes. Mum checks the meat.

Reckless in my confusion, in my shock: 'Mum, you can't look after her here in your dugout.'

'I can, Fabienne, and I will.'

Silence. I am desperate to reverse everything that has happened.

'Well, what about if I come back to Coober Pedy to help . . .? What about if . . .?'

'You are not giving up your life in Adelaide!'

'But I don't even like it very much, there's nothing for me down in Adelaide. I want to be here to help. I feel useless, like there's nothing I can do . . .'

'That's right, there is nothing you can do.' She slams down her knife. 'You're going back to Adelaide. You're not coming back to this dust bowl, you're not coming back to Coober Pedy and, besides, you'd drive me up the wall if you shifted back home. You know that two grown women living under the same roof is impossible!'

'Yes, but . . .' and with this my mum gets impatient.

'No buts, Fabienne. Nana is staying with me. I have been living here long enough. She is here in Coober Pedy and she is my mother and I will look after her till the day she dies if necessary. Just like her mother and her mother's mother. Just like my daughters will look after me. It is life and will be like this until the end of time, at least for this family.'

My mind is swirling with arguments. I can't say anything.

'She's not going into a home, Fabienne.'

'Yes, I know that, Mum!' I am appalled at the very suggestion. I am appalled at my mother even thinking that I would consider such a thing. Images of my mother in old age confront me. I push them to the back of my mind. We will cross that bridge when we come to it.

'But it's not fair that you should have to look after her. It's not fair that Nana should be like this. She's not even seventy. It's not fair that other people's relatives live twice as long, and they're not half as nice as—'

'I know it's not fair, but that's life, Fub. Sometimes life's not fair.'

There is nothing else to say. There is nothing else I can do.

I miss Nana already, her advice and support, her telephone calls. I can't imagine life without her, and her voice on the line every Sunday.

Someone suggests that my Nana might be quite enjoying time travelling between the past and the present. Perhaps it's Nana's turn, once again, to be the child. I'm not sure. What I do know is it's time for me to keep the faith, maintain the flow of love. It's up to me to provide support and strength, to give advice and accept that it may never be taken notice of. To be all accepting and see the spirit of Nana beyond her inability to speak clearly, to read and to initiate conversation. Beyond all the expectations society puts on people to be 'normal' and 'healthy'.

My Nana had a stroke. I'm given advice by friends. Well-meaning, sympathetic, yet intrusive. Every grandparent dies at some point of our existence. It's a fact of life. And death. People are sympathetic, but I'm considered fortunate to have known my Nana for so long. Even at all, in fact. Some people never get to know their grandparents. Some people never get to know their parents. I thank all for their advice, for the sense of perspective. Everything is supposed to have perspective when seen from a distance. But perspective does nothing to ease the shock on impact. Perspective doesn't ease the pain. Perspective does nothing to ease me. Distance does nothing either.

I'm looking down from that plane once again, but this time I'm in my lounge room at home. I can hear the sea outside. This time I'm looking into the fractals of life, my life.

Shock is like a whole new landscape. A whole new moonscape. I'm in the same familiar place but the rules are different. The fractals are not quite the same, and I need to figure them out or accept them, like the different things that life brings to me, the different patterns and knots I try to unravel.

I'm thinking of other ways to go home. I'm thinking, there must be other ways I can try.

Parliament House

Canberra is a bubble protecting itself from the rest of the nation. It sits within itself, a series of concentric circles overlapping like ripples in a pond created by naughty boys chucking rocks at innocent tadpoles from great heights. And Parliament House is the bubble within the bubble, vacuum-sealed from reality. An imaginary fairy castle, a glass palace within a wonderland of self-delusion and story-making. The tales are darker and more complex than those imagined yet defy truth. It is up to you to decide whether this one is real. It might be. It might not . . .

The first day at Parliament House a man sits opposite me, in the tea room, dunks his biscuit and says, 'Ah, yes . . . you're the Aborigine.'

He smiles and sucks.

'I have a name.' I look at him. 'Are you in Economics?'

Further down the table someone says, 'Nice cuppa tea we're having.'

After the tea break, I sit in the office overlooking the American Embassy. I can see the whole block has been built in a pseudo-American style. Like stepping back through time when Kentucky Fried Chicken actually had eleven herbs and spices and 'The Brady Bunch' was prime-time viewing. I wonder if the American Embassy sprouts fake snowdrifts during Thanksgiving. If it does, it would fit with the fairytale reality of this bubble city.

Such beautiful buildings in this city and I can't find a place to rent.

On the other side of Parliament House is the Eagle, and the defence base. Hmmm . . . We are surrounded. Good thing I'm camping in a kombi. No one would bother to bug it. Can't say these things out loud. People will think I am mad.

Looking out. I wonder if someone's looking back.

The phone rings.

I wonder if this is bugged? I think. Probably . . . definitely.

'Parliament Research Operations, Indigenous Department . . . Oh, good morning, sir.'

'Give me the latest figures on Aboriginal mortality.'

'Anything specific?'

'No . . . and I need them in the next five minutes.'

'Yes, sir.'

'Oh, wait . . . tell me this . . . Is it three out of five Aboriginal children who die before they reach three years of age, or two out of five?'

'Five out of eight Aboriginal children die before the age of three, sir.'

'Five out of eight?'

'Yes, sir.'

'And these are the latest figures?'

'As of the last census, direct from the Bureau of Statistics, sir.'

'And being Aboriginal yourself, would you say these figures are true?'

'The statistics are correct.'

'Right. That'll fix that bastard for Aboriginal Rights at question time.'

'It's terrible,' looking out of the window, watching the embassy watching.

'It's a perfect example of how tax payers' money is being wasted! Fax me the figures straightaway.'

'Yes.'

'Oh, and come down here and explain to me why these women don't want a bridge built to the island.'

'Which island do you mean, sir?'

'What do you mean, which island? Bloody Hindmarsh Island of course! None of the women want to discuss the matter with me. It's outrageous. I'm losing my credibility.'

'I'll be at your office as soon as I can, sir.'

'Good,' he says and the line cuts out.

As I walk down the immaculate corridors of our 'nation's engine room' I'm thinking about what to say to this politician. I'm preparing in my mind the words I need to say and I'm thinking about the things I can't.

How do you explain to a politician the life of an Aboriginal person? What use are statistics? The politicians only use them as weapons to throw at each other. Point scoring.

Shoes tap down the empty corridor.

How do you try and explain the intricacies of a people bereft of trust, of support, imprisoned, reviled by the wider community and dispossessed of their culture to a person who doesn't even have to worry about money?

The parquetry floors gleam with fresh polish. The shine reminds me of the hospital floor back in Coober Pedy but there is no dust here. Soft carpets glow pale, pristine.

How can you explain that the land and the people are one, when the politicians can't look past statistics, when they can't look beyond the slogans to the very meaning of the words?

The land and the people are one. Aboriginal communities do not want another man-made structure weighing upon their backs.

But the reality is that most people don't see it that

way. They say, 'Bloody Abos, they're just as bad as the greenies. It's only a bridge, what's the fuss?'

If it is only a bridge, why is it so important to build it? But I don't know. Maybe I'm just lost. Looking for meaning in the wrong places.

If people are going to be willing to drive for an hour and a half from Adelaide to get to Hindmarsh Island, I don't think an extra fifteen minutes waiting for the ferry to cross is going to bother them.

What is the fuss? Is it because an impoverished state government made a bad financial decision and needed to find a scapegoat? Was the state government looking to big daddy federal government to bail it out? Maybe the bridge is too expensive not to build (lawyers are cunning bastards).

All of these thoughts flood my mind as I walk the 'hallowed halls' of Parliament. This fairyland palace. More art hangs from these walls than in the National Gallery. Occasionally there is an Aboriginal piece.

The media love to kick a dog when it's down.

Turn the corner to track down another long empty corridor.

Who is more down than the black dog of the Aboriginal community? But I'm not supposed to have such radical thoughts while I'm here. Maybe it's all in my head.

Near the shadow ministry the paintings fade away and shutters are closed against the sun. The abundance of funds is concentrated nearer to the offices of those in power.

One of the first rules of war is to divide and conquer. They tried that.

Starve and isolate a group of people long enough and they will fight amongst themselves. The human drive is to survive, no matter what race, no matter what culture. How do you explain this to a politician?

I am not allowed to give an opinion, only facts, I remind myself. But what happens when the facts are buried under a history of whitewash? What happens when the media don't present the facts because they are not entertaining enough for the populace? They don't want to lose their ratings now. Don't want to lose sales. The dollar is always the bottom line, isn't it? I straighten my shirt, push my hair back. Knock on the door.

'Ah, yes, come in.'

'Here are the statistics you requested, sir.'

'Take a seat.'

'I've highlighted the relevant information.'

'Now, tell me what you know about Hindmarsh Island.'

How can I explain? Never cross an Aboriginal woman. Never expect trust. How can they trust you after all they have been through? They've had their children taken away. They've been pushed from their homes. They've been split up from their families, been deprived of their history.

'I'm not Ngarrandjeri, sir. You would need to speak to the people involved.'

'I've tried but they won't discuss it with me. I was practically attacked by one of them last week.'

Of course they're angry, I think, but I don't say it. 'You are a government representative, sir.'

'Ah, I am in opposition, not government.'

'Nonetheless, they see you as a representative of Parliament.'

'Hmmm.' He leans back on his chair, puts his hands behind his head.

'The only thing I can suggest is keeping a respectful distance, sir.' Don't look at his eyes. Keep your eyes to the floor. Stay standing. Hands behind the back.

They're holding on to what's left as hard and as tight as they can. Now they're expected to expose what's left of their culture to justify themselves. You might as well ask them to be subjected to a cavity search and have it filmed on 'Sixty Minutes'. But you can't say these words in Parliament House. Too emotional.

'Let me explain my political position to you,' says the politician. 'There are some members around who believe you should all still be on missions.'

'Oh.'

'There are some who even say the missions were too good for you.' He leans forward, staring for a reaction.

This is way out of my league. This is way too much for me.

'Perhaps a conciliatory approach would be best?' I suggest.

'And how do you propose I do that?'

'I'm sorry, sir, I can't help you there. I'm afraid I'll have to be returning to my office now.'

'Yes, well, I'll read those statistics when I've got time.' He's dismissive and places the information amongst the paper mountain on his desk.

There is nothing else for me to do, there is nothing else for me to say. Click, click, back along the empty corridors.

There is, of course, plenty for me to say and do but I'd be strung up and slaughtered as a mad woman. In Parliament House nothing is supposed to make sense. And of course I probably imagined the whole thing. I'm not thinking straight since Nana's stroke. Don't take my word for it. You can never trust an Aboriginal woman's word anyway. It's best just to keep some things to yourself. Secret.

How Black Are You?

One day at Mabel's house the police knock on her front door. The kids crowd around. A young white man with cropped hair and a smart khaki shirt and a short man wearing a pale blue shirt and navy tie stride through the passageway. The sergeant knocks at the open kitchen door and yells over the noise of the radio. 'Hello?' Behind him his officer clutches a brown briefcase. They walk into the small kitchen to find a group of adults sitting around an old scrubbed table drinking tea.

The officer places a few papers on the table.

'Now everybody,' he says to the adults. 'We need some information.'

Four or five people sit and look at the papers. All of them have dark skin. The colour of clay. The kids are shooed out to the backyard, happy and noisy. The house is clean, the yard is neat.

The oldest woman, Aunty Agnes, gets up and turns off the radio. The music stops abruptly and leaves a gap in the air. Red dust stirred up by kids playing outside wafts in to fill in the silence.

'We need to know which of you are working,' says the tall sergeant. He stands solid and talks too loud.

'And we need to know which of you will sign this form.' He places his hands on the table.

Old dark Aunty Agnes, slight in her cotton dress and greying hair, picks up the paper, squints and calls, 'Mabel! May!'

Mabel walks in with her swag of kids behind her. The little ones crowd around her legs and smile at the police sergeant in his pressed khaki shirt and neat trousers. He frowns and doesn't look at the papers. They read 'Identification of Aboriginality'. They are presigned in bright blue pen.

A couple of the men get up from the table and go out to the backyard and start yelling at the kids to get in the ute.

Mabel is fresh in a cool dress. She sees the police sergeant and looks at the papers on the table.

'G'day, May.'

'Hello, Greg. How are you today?' The words friendly, the tone cool.

'Not bad, May. Just a bit of paperwork to sort out. Doesn't really concern you though.'

Mabel picks up one of the papers. 'This to do with the dog licence, Greg? You not taking our kids away are you, mate?'

'Look, Mabel, it's just paperwork and you know it doesn't affect you. I'm just asking these people to fill out these forms now.'

Aunty Agnes looks at Mabel. The room is silent in contrast with the men outside now yelling louder at the kids. Frantic.

'This is my family. Anything that concerns them concerns me. You know that.'

Greg looks at the floor. Mabel shoves the papers into the police officer's chest. 'You know we're all black.'

Greg doesn't answer.

'You know that every adult in this house works, Officer,' Mabel says.

Silence.

'We're not signing that.' Greg does not look at her.

'You gonna take these kids away cause we're black?'

'Look, Mabel, this doesn't concern you.'

'It concerns my family. Any business of my family is mine.' Mabel looks him in the eye. It's quiet out in the yard now.

'Just tell me you're not Abo. That's all,' says the other officer.

The children have evaporated from around Mabel's legs.

'You know where I work, Greg.'

'You're a cleaner up at the hospital. Yeah, I know that.'

The sidekick with the tie writes this down.

'You know we all work,' says Mabel.

'Yeah, I know that.'

'You know who I am,' says Mabel quietly.

Greg nods and looks at the floor. 'Yeah, I know that you're—'

Aunty Agnes pushes back her chair and stands up. Her dark eyes stare at the officer. Her hand steadies on the old kitchen table. Dark clay.

'Aunty Ag.' Mabel softly gestures to the old woman to sit down, then turns back to the police officer.

'Well, you know we're not signing that.' And she walks over to put the kettle back on the stove. She needs another cuppa. She needs a smoke but she's not lighting up till the cops leave. She turns her back on the men. Aunty Agnes turns on the radio.

With that the sergeant nods, 'May.' And they leave.

The front door slams and Aunty Agnes says, 'Is that fella blind or stupid or what?'

Mabel turns and says, 'So where did the fellas take the kids?' She turns back to the window and wonders if and when the police will be back. 'How much further do I have to travel?' she thinks.

There's nowhere else for her to go.

Time To Go Looking

Sometimes I feel like a door between two rooms, a fence dividing two pieces of land, two countries, two universes.

'Are you really black?' says a blackfella, his eyes narrowing. 'Or do you just want our money?'

'Yes, I'm black.'

'Okay, prove it.'

But I can't peel back my skin like stripping paint. I can't say 'go talk to that rellie over there' because what if my family doesn't know where we are from? What if nobody talks about it? What if it's covered up, like the silt on the riverbed floor? What then?

'You know, it's people like you who give me the shits, saying your great-aunt twice removed from your father's side is Aboriginal. Then you think you can say you're Aboriginal too. How black are you, anyway?'

says a whitefella, his eyes narrowing. 'Or are you just after our money?'

As if I could show them shades of grey, like colour charts. I feel like folding out the family album. Like I'm hauling out my family credentials. Have it engraved on the family silver. Hah.

'I'm black.'

I am all one colour. I speak two languages but they are the same. I feel like the translator. I feel like the fence-sitter.

So where do I come from? Who does this face belong to? Time to go looking. Time to go looking . . .

Home

'Hi, honey, how was work today?' he asks. The kombi provides a cocoon from the madness of Parliament. It's weird, but it's real. We head out to the camp where we are living on the edge of town.

'I want to go home.' We rumble past the neatly placed suburbs. The little Lego towns.

'Time to go back to Adelaide?' I nod but think, I need to go *home*. But where is that? Is Adelaide still home? After all of this? Where is home? Is this dispossessed?

'Let's run away from this place while we still can. You know Canberra, it's not normal. It's not natural,' he says. We weave our way through the circular roads running rings around themselves.

'Yeah, but where is?' I ask and sigh. We park our kombi next to a creek bed. Just above it sits a besser-brick toilet block. The sign next to the toilet block reads, 'Camping for more than 48 hours is prohibited.'

'Tell me all about it,' he says.

'I want to go looking.'

'Looking for what.'

Where do I begin? 'Home.'

'Home?'

'I wanna go up north. Find out where Nana came from.'

'Alright.' He shrugs. 'The kombi will make it.' Smiles. 'Yeah, no worries. We can do it.'

'Yeah, but I wanna go it alone.'

'I'll follow you.'

'You've already followed me here.'

'We can do it together.' He almost shouts. He is excited.

I want to say, hey this isn't your journey. This isn't yours. But I know I can't and won't because it will hurt him. Because he won't understand. And it's not because he's white. I feel ashamed for thinking that. It would hurt because if it was him looking for his country I would want to come too. And if he said no to me? I just wouldn't listen.

Dizzy, confused. Feel like I'm going to be sick.

'You should just go home.' I rub my face. Try to massage the ache from my eyes.

'My home is with you.' He pulls my hands from my face.

Well, I'd *better* find out where I am from then. But I don't say it.

'You can come with me to Sydney. It's just me from then on.' I look him in the eye.

'Alright,' he says. Face to face. He doesn't smile. I can see he's thinking about the challenge ahead.

Under the camping sign red letters spell out, 'Heavy fines will be incurred.'

This Isn't Your History

'Are you a history student?' asks the librarian.

'No, not really.'

'Member of staff, researcher? At which university?' The librarian picks up a pen to fill in a form.

'No. I'm not at any university at the moment.'

'Can I ask what you're looking for?'

'Yep, we're here to find material about the Bundjalung region, Northern New—'

'Yes, I know where it is. You do realise we have quite a substantial holding of information on that region here?' Pen goes down. Why do librarians always peer over their reading glasses? 'Which we would expect, given this is the Institute of Aboriginal and Islander Studies. That's why we are here actually.'

'Well, I could print out a list of references relating to the area.'

'That would be great.'

'It will be quite expensive though.' There is a glint of mocking in his eyes. He is smirking.

'How much, do you think?'

'Oh, it would be over fifty dollars at least . . .'

'No problem. When do you think you could print it by? It's just that we're only in Canberra for a few more days.'

With this there is a significant change in attitude.

'So you're really serious about this request. I'm sorry, could you please explain to me what exactly you are doing.'

If we keep it simple it will avoid further confusion.

'We're looking for material on the Bundjalung area and we don't actually have very long to stay in Canberra to find this information. And I am actually telling you the truth, we are actually seriously looking for information on that area. Actually.'

'But you're not with an institution of any kind?'

'No, we are not, and that kombi out there is what we have been sleeping in. And given that it is forecast minus one tonight and the institute is heated, maybe it would be more efficient if we slept in here? I also know the head librarian. She's on leave, isn't she?' Looking around.

'Well, why didn't you say so in the first place. What area did you say you were looking for?'

'B-u-n-d-j-a-l-u-n-g. Clarence River.'

My Ashlyn May

I had tried to find out about the community my grandfather came from. Wodenbong Mission. I did not have the money to travel further on. I felt bad about it, but I tried to read something in the history of it. I couldn't go looking on the land, so I went looking through the library. It's what I had been taught. Like a good little history student. I had been taught like a good little Aborigine.

Classified Information

RECNO   0058132
CALLNO   MF 12
AUTHOR   'Classified'
TITLE   Bundjalung social organisation
PUB   Sydney
DATE   1959
COLLTN   254 pp
SERIES   Thesis for PhD, University of Sydney
NOTES   maps, tables
ANNOT

Bandjalang tribes as a social unit, including major internal subdivisions, population movements. Contacts before and after the arrival of Europeans. Includes relations with the white group. Description of clan as a local marriage group. Description as a religious group. Local grouping today. Gossip groups, activities. Kinship—terminology, behaviour, sections. Indigenous marriage. Marital status of females. Stability of marriage. List of clans. Abortions and miscarriages. Warfare.

Table showing locality, clan name, dialect, including main surnames of today.

Paper showing why Bandjalang have remained an unassimilated minority and effect of white contact on their social organisation.

Field work done at Tabulam and Wodenbong.

'I'd like a copy of this manuscript, please.'

The institute librarian looks at the highlighted list. 'I really don't think you should be reading that.'

'Why?'

'It's restricted information.'

'Restricted? In what sense?'

'It's sensitive material. Classified.'

'But it was included in the listings you gave us for Bundjalung material.'

'Yes, I know that.'

'Well, you understand that is the research project I'm working on? It's my family history.'

'Yes. I can appreciate that.'

'Well, these papers have maps of Wodenbong Mission.'

'Yes.'

'That is where my grandfather came from, you know, where he was born. Well, this says it has a map of the house he may have lived in.'

'So it does.' The librarian hands back the list.

'Well, I'd like to read it, please.'

'I'm sorry, but that map holds personal information. It may be sensitive. It may contradict information that you have about your family. It is institute policy not to release personal and/or potentially sensitive material to the general public without the author's permission.'

'But I'm not the general public! That's my

grandfather's community there! It's information about my *immediate* family.'

'That's exactly why you can't have it.'

'Okay,' trying to calm down. 'Who do I need to get permission from, regarding this document?'

'From the author.'

'So is it possible for the institute to contact the author on my behalf?'

'Yes?'

'Great! Can you do that?'

'No.'

'Why?'

'The author of that particular manuscript is very ill at the moment.'

'So what do you do when an author is ill, or dead for that matter?'

'Well, it's policy for the institute to contact the next of kin . . .' The librarian says this vaguely, as if he is not really sure.

'And in this case that might be . . .?'

'His daughter.'

'What's her phone number?'

'She lives in Canada,' she says without missing a beat.

The quietness of the library and the musty smell of institutionalised papers, books, newspapers, gently decomposing, fading over time, fills my sinuses, my mind. Within the largest collection of Aboriginal-related material in the southern hemisphere, no, in the world, I am marooned. The white anthropologist who collected the material of my family, of my ancestors, has greater right of access than I do. It is his work. It is his information. I am dispossessed of it. Another gate has been locked. I wonder how many other people have come into this great institute, this wonderful cornucopia of information, and gone away empty-handed.

Grimly smiling, I walk away from the librarian, restraining myself, understanding that he is only doing his job, he is only following policy.

I take my partner aside and say, 'We've got three days. Photocopy what you can . . . Don't show it to the librarian.'

His pale face looks bewildered but he nods and he sneaks things to the photocopier. We take notes behind bookshelves.

People build gates. People jump over them. At five o'clock the library closes and we are ushered out the door.

I sit on the front step of the entrance. Can't stop crying.

'What's wrong?'

'I don't know. It just seems so weird, so over-whelming.' I smear the tears on my shirt sleeve.

'You worried what your Nana's gonna say?' He passes me a hankie.

Blow. 'No, not really. I want to surprise her, I suppose.' We sit and watch the light turn grey.

'Gonna be a cold one tonight.'

'Yeah . . .' I say. 'Feel a bit sick actually.'

'You'll be right. Probably all the preservatives they put in the books.'

'Preservatives?'

'Yeah, so they don't decompose while you're reading them. You probably breathed in too many stuffy chemicals.' We laugh. 'No dinner for you then, mate.' He pulls me off the verandah. We walk away from the building to our home, parked on the bitumen.

'I feel like some fish actually.'

'Fish, in Canberra? This is an inland city. You'll be pushing it! C'mon, let me drive you to Sydney.'

'But only to Sydney, mind.'

'If you want fish,' he says. 'Look no further.'

Accidental Archives

There are some beautiful archives and libraries in Sydney, rich in life, history, unfulfilled ideas and details of people intertwined through words, forms and untitled documents. But the beauty is not in the furniture, nor in the décor. You have to find it, or fall over it.

I sit under the fluorescent lighting of the archive, in its airtight room, trembling lest the fragile paper fall apart.

30th April, 1908

From: Police Station Maclean

To: Aboriginal Protectorate, NSW

Sergeant Thompson reports that a number of the parents of European children attending the Maclean Public School do object to the Aboriginal children being allowed to attend.

The Sergeant thinks it would be a great benefit to the Aboriginal children, if a school was established on Ulgundahi Island. They are a sober and respectful lot and are anxious that their children should learn . . .

Mr Robert Gall, Head Teacher, visited the island yesterday and selected a site of one acre of unoccupied land, which is well situated and on high ground.

The Sergeant has no doubt that a few other families will take up their residence on this Island if allowed. The present occupants are very fond of the island, as the system of allowing them about 3 acres each of good land, to cultivate their own way, seems to agree with their nature rather than cultivating the farm as a whole.

Attached is a list of the Aborigines on the Island . . .

I find my great-great-grandfather's cross, petitioning to apply for 'The Establishment of a Provisional School at Ulgundahi'. Under the pledge 'that our children shall attend the said school regularly and punctually'. The inspector sergeant has written 'Jack Freeburn—his mark', and across from this is a listing of my great-grandmother 'Amy Freeburn—aged five'.

It is the first written confirmation of my family's life on the island. It is an accident of history, a mistake of misfiling, that I am able to see this rotting piece of paper because it is inconsequential, it has wasted valuable filing space for years and should've have been thrown out long ago.

It was only found because the librarian behind the counter happened to have the same name as myself and made the extra effort to look beyond the boundaries of my listed request.

To keep a list of lowly Aboriginal people asking for a little school to be built, in order to be kept away from the whites, would be inefficient. Aboriginal history is not written history, and personal papers such as these have been thrown out, scribbled over or burned. It, along with other crumbling pieces, has been clogging up the archives. In this day and age such a list would've been thrown out with the weekly recycling.

It is my great-great-grandfather's mark.

Attached to this list is an ink sketch of the island. Dotted on it are the houses divided up for the people living on the island.

The Freeburn referred to in the following information was an aboriginal. It was common practice to call aborigines after well-known white people . . .

Each house is given a name taken from the white history of the area. Cameron, Sailor, Flauders, Blackeney, Freeburn. Each Aboriginal person is 'given' the name of the house they live in as their last name. They are advised to forget their 'black names', to forget their language.

I'm reading these historical papers found. I stare at a dot, the soaking of ink on the paper. The dot on the page represents the beginning of the white name and the ending of the Bundjalung one. It pins the people to the house. It pins them down . . .

There were certain days when the men from the Aboriginal Protection Board would visit the island. The bigger boys and girls used to plant (hide). They'd say 'He's comin to get me, he's comin to take me away.' Manys the time my father would have words with the Welfare who were out to take children from our family and many other families as well. I remember my brother got taken away when he was a boy . . .

. . . a small dot on the landscape . . .

Though the nomadic urge is strong . . . the equally inherent quality of love for the district in which he is born and has been reared is doubtless a strong asset in the conduct of the stations, for the native Australian learns to know and love every ridge and hollow and tree and bend, every waterhole and little patch of scrub that is associated with his boyhood and young manhood, and once he has overcome the desire to wander from Government supervision, the task of keeping him at home becomes easier year by year as the surface of the country outside the settlement changes with the advance of the white men.

. . . when the darkness should've spread, seeped over the boundaries of the island into the river and covered the entire land . . .

I look around these quiet stuffy rooms to see if anybody can detect the violence of my thoughts.

Everyone's face is down, reading, slightly jaundiced in the yellow light. I wipe the tears from my face lest they fall and ruin these papers I hold.

'You're crying too much, honey,' I hear someone whisper. I smile to myself. 'Crying too much.'

'Well, give me a better reason to cry. And besides, I thought you were going to show me where to eat fish.'

'Fish, fish. Bloody fish.' The archive staff frown at us. No talking allowed.

Out in the warm air. 'Right, show me one of those restaurants where you can pick yourself out a live crab.'

'I thought you were vegetarian, remember?'

'Alright. How about fish 'n' chips instead? We walk down the steps into Sydney's CBD. 'How far is Newcastle from here?'

Dolphins

Blurred by the blue sea and the Yamba beer I try writing again.

The dolphins are swimming, blue-grey eyes smiling, skin shining through the murky blue, swirling sand, a flick of the tail, gliding and weaving through the water. Blue-grey they dive, weaving the fabric of the sea into the river, through the river, over the sandbar, across the edge of the world into the green continent. Weaving the bright blue sea-fabric with the murky green-brown of the river. Back and forth the dolphins swim, gliding the fabric of colour from their tales. Crossing the boundaries of sea and earth until the river and the sea cannot be divided. The landscape dripping, green, wet, warm and lazy. A wide blue oil slick smoothing away the grey gristle inside you, the grit from your brain. Moving inland the dolphins weave their translucent message.

We have come from a place of clay and rivers, a place where trees once outnumbered people. Where the land and its people were one. *Where the land and its people are one.*

I went looking, Ashlyn. I went looking for the island. I pretended to look for the signposts in the historical papers I found along the way . . .

The Northern Rivers area is hemmed in on three sides by rugged mountains and on the fourth side by the sea. The

Clarence is up to mile wide and has 99 islands within it banks ...

The land consisted of sub-tropical rainforest, which included dense rich red cedar trees, ferns, vines, stinging nettles and yams.

Its climate is mainly temperate, mildly-humid and frost free (except in the foothills and mountains). Rainfall approximates 50 inches each year and as such there is no shortage of water. The abundant rainfall feeds the river, estuaries, broadwater and coastal swamps.

Floods are a feature of life of the great rivers ... and during the previous century at least four serious floods occurred in the last decade.

The balance between water, vegetation and fauna was to be upset dramatically by white invasion ...

I went looking, Ashlyn. If I said to you that we came from the dolphins at the edge of the world, you would think I was some sort of crazed hippy. Freaked-out on too much vegetarian food. Too many lentils, you would think. That I'd taken this 'new age' stuff just a bit too far. 'Here, get some beef into ya,' our family says to each other. 'Eat meat, it's only natural. You look anaemic.' You, Ashlyn, who is yet to discover the pleasures of a blood-encrusted bone, cooked especially with the roast dinner. Drooling, mouth watering. You would look to the others for confirmation of my madness. They, depending on what mood they were in, would either agree that I am strange, or they would say, 'It's true, listen.'

My family would nod sagely and give you cryptic looks, like rolling sheep eyes.

Trust me to go looking now. But then again I always did things the most difficult way.

I had to read those books, about our country, about our land.

When sawyers and squatters moved into the coastal land between the Clarence River and Queensland in the 1830s several thousand Aborigines were already living in the region . . .

The Australian aborigines can be classed as indolent and the Clarence River contingent was no exception . . . Food in abundance was obtainable without toil and with little effort or energy. The scrubs abounded with paddymelons, bandicoots, opossums, snakes, lizards, grubs, turkeys, pigeons and yams. The open country was plentifully supplied with kangaroos and wallabies. The swamps provided an endless variety of game, including ducks, geese, swans and coots. The rivers and creeks were teaming with fish. A couple of hours work would be sufficient.

My family would tell you the meaning of the dolphins, of where we came from.

I went looking for this island, this river. Dearest

Ashlyn, sometimes I felt I went looking in all the wrong places.

Lighthouse

'Can I help?' the voice behind the Newcastle Council Chambers counter asks.

'Yes. I'm looking for a place called the Lighthouse.'

In 1922 there are no drugs to ease labour pain. At least not at the Lighthouse. Only prayer. A white nurse whispers encouragement over my Great-Grandmother Amy Freeburn as the labour pains swell and stretch inside of her ... She's sweating and moaning with each tide.

'We have a number of lighthouses in Newcastle. Which one were you after in particular?'

'Well, actually it's not a lighthouse as such, it's a building that used to be a hospital for the Salvation Army.'

Can you imagine the pains rippling through Amy Freeburn's body?

'Did you ask the Salvation Army where it is?'

'Yes, they suggested I contact the history officer here at the council.'

'I'm afraid the history officer is on leave for two weeks. Can you come back then?'

Amy's away from her people, removed from her land.

'Well, we've actually travelled here on a research project and I was hoping somebody could help me now.'

'You could try the library, or you could ring the Salvation Army headquarters. But I'm sorry, we can't help you at the moment.'

Our great-grandmother is alone in the hospital, where those blackened by original sin can come and give birth. Without judgement.

If anybody came with Amy Freeburn to ease her through the birth, I do not know. If anybody held Amy as the pains pushed out Mabel, I do not know. Others did know but they couldn't say.

Great-Great-Grandpa Freeburn

The day Mabel Louise Freeburn was born, her grandfather knew by the glint in the dolphins' eyes. The dolphins had crossed the edge of the world to tell Jack Freeburn that she was born. He was fishing from the Clarence River. It was the sign of new life that caught his eye. He pondered life, his life, his river and how everything had changed so fast in his lifetime.

Archaeological evidence shows their ancestors had been there for at least four thousand five hundred years, and that inter-trading had gone on for more than a millennium . . .

Jack Freeburn knew his language. He was a respected man of his community, yet his community was dissolving.

As the white man's hunt for red cedar spread north from Sydney . . . the Bundjalung found their homeland occupied.

The white man's voice did not echo his own. It did not speak for his people.

The Statements of many writers and speakers throughout Australia to the effect that the Government is not carrying out its obligations towards the aboriginals is not borne out as a result of a visit by a representative of the Daily Examiner *to the aboriginal station on Ullagundahi Island.*

People were dying before they were ready. His land was changing and the river would not share its secrets any more. He knew his language but he could not speak it. He could be punished. It burned and blistered, unspoken on his tongue.

On this station there is every evidence of the 75 aboriginals, representing 3 generations, living a happy, care-free family life, with the advantages of civilised conditions, combined with a specially prepared set of conditions, which make for the minimum restraint on the natural inclinations of the native mind.

Jack Freeburn knew his land but he could not live on it. He could not walk his country according to the laws and the rules of his own people. He could not sustain his family according to the cycle of the seasons. He could not walk as a free man. Instead he was allowed an island in the middle of a river. His one sanctuary. Something that could be called home in this break-down of his world, but only if he tilled it, turned it, lived from it, ate off it, according to white man's rule.

The island, between Maclean and Harwood, is in charge of Mr AE Cameron, as manager under the Aborigines Protection Board.

Cameron was a good enough man in his own way, Jack thought. Kind-hearted and well-meaning. But he was just a white man. And he knew nothing of the river. Didn't know how to fish.

Another fallacy that is exploded by a visit to the island is the oft repeated statement that the aboriginal of Australia cannot stand up to hard work or the plodding, steady, continuous cultivation of the land, though it is admitted that he requires continuous supervision by the white man to bring his efforts to fruition.

Jack Freeburn ate the food he grew from his own island, he fished from its shores. He ate his own island. He had to eat the earth he walked on, over and over again.

On Ulgundahi Island are men who not only do their own farming but cut their own cane, and go out amongst the other cane-cutting gangs on equal terms with all-comers . . . as general farming assistants.

Jack Freeburn began to keep the laws to himself. He had to. 'There is no one to share them with any more,' he thought. Great-Great-Grandpa Freeburn stared deep into the water to find answers. The dolphins rising to the surface to meet his gaze broke through his thoughts with a message of new life. A life to shine in his from now on. The light of his granddaughter, born at that very moment hundreds of miles away, down south in the grey, clotted, smoky city.

'There did used to be a hospital in Newcastle, or a maternity home for single mothers, run by nuns, but it was torn down years ago. It was called the Lighthouse, or the House of Light. Hang on. I'll see if we've got any photos.'

Mabel Louise Freeburn was born pink, small and wet amongst the grey of the coal-mining town. She was born far from the island, from the greens and blues of her country.

'No, there are no photos.'

'Were any of the records kept? You know, from the hospital? Births, deaths?'

If Amy had been forced to go to Newcastle to give birth, I do not know.

Full bloods, half-bloods, quadroons, octaroons and others ... assured the Daily Examiner *representative that they were quite happy with their families.*

Mabel Louise Freeburn never knew her father. He was white. He would not own up.

'Most hospitals didn't keep statistics on their Aboriginal patients,' says the librarian. 'Try the New South Wales Archives.'

Amy and her baby would be home soon, back to the island. The green landscape would circle around them and become the womb of their universe, the river an umbilical cord to the edge of the world, to the dolphins.

Great-Great-Grandpa Freeburn pulled in his fishing line. He would not compete with the dolphins today. Leave them to their fish and their river in peace. How could he compete with the messengers of birth? A birth so far away, off his tribal land, yet within his blood. He left his granddaughter's totem to weave the silks of the river to and from the sea.

This message of Mabel's birth was passed on through the dolphins. Nana told me this so matter-of-factly, how could I not believe her? It is harder to believe that someone could walk on water. It is harder to believe that the world is round when it falls off from the land in a wash of pale translucent blue.

It is harder to believe that no one else could know.

The Newcastle Council fountain spurts and sputters. I watch the soft arc of water.

'Need to go to the loo.'

'Well, go on then.'

But I don't move from the seat outside the library. I look around the deserted park. Everyone is inside. 'How can I feel so cold when the sun is shining?'

'Shall we go and get something to eat?' he says. 'Bit of food will warm you up. Then we could go back into the library, maybe keep looking.'

'What for? There's nothing in there,' I say.

'C'mon, there'll be something in the family archives. Births, deaths, marriages. We'll keep hassling the librarian. Get her to ring the history officer.'

'You forget. We didn't get recorded. You had to be white and well off to rate a mention in those days.' I stand up and the park sways and swims.

'Whoa, you alright?'

'Yeah, feel a bit hot and stuffy, that's all.' Walk over to the fountain. 'Let's go to the beach.'

'Minute ago you were complaining it was cold.'

'Will you just get off my back!'

'What! What did I say wrong now?'

'Don't you get it? There's nothing here! Don't you understand? She was black. No one gives a fuck! You don't care. You're just along for the ride. Perhaps I should've just got a road map. This is just a bloody magical mystery tour for you!'

'Oh, fuck off! You think this is fun for me? Watching you waltz around the place, crying here, crying there. Do you think I enjoy pandering to your whims and crazy ideas. You've lost it, honey. You're off in the Dreamtime.'

'Don't you use that word like that. What do you know about Dreamtime. What would you know about all of this? Hey?'

We are screaming at each other. The fountain keeps spouting in a lazy arc behind us, almost silent, sulking.

'I know that this is the here and now. You can't get the past back just by looking it up in books. Why don't you go and talk to your Nana? How would she feel about you fucking around with her past like this? Does she know? You can't keep driving around like this. Just going from here to there.'

'Don't you tell me what to do with my Nana. What the fuck would you know?'

But there's a violent stop to the argument. Lunge forward and throw up. Hold on to the fountain. Keep head down. Wait for the next wave. This ain't surfing.

'Shit. Honey-bun, you alright?' He steps around the mess on the lawn. Leans down to hold back my hair.

'I don't fucking need this.'

'Look, I'm sorry. C'mon, let's get you to the van.'

'Fuck you. I'm taking the bus.'

'Oh, c'mon. Where are you going to get a bus to Grafton from here?'

'I can get one from Sydney.'

'But this is bloody Newcastle. You're going the wrong way!'

'You're just a fucking white man and you will *never* understand!'

Scream at him across the park. Shock.

'Oh god. I can't believe I said that.' I burst into tears.

'I'm sorry. I'm sorry.' But he's already walking to the parking lot.

'Let me do this. Please.'

'Sure,' he says, revving the engine.

'I just don't know what's got into me.'

His face is impassive.

All the way back to Sydney we pretend the engine noise stops us from talking. Though it hasn't before. The Sydney bus depot seems enormous and overwhelming compared to the clapped-out Coober Pedy bus stop. People sit, lined up against the walls, waiting for their bus, staring straight ahead.

We hug.

'Thank you.' But he doesn't say anything. 'It's probably just hormones. I've never felt so premenstrual in all my life. I'm sorry I'm like this.'

He doesn't say anything.

Smile and wave from the window of the bus.

He doesn't wave back.

'Next stop, Grafton.' Trying not to fall asleep.

Sleep

On the bus I sleep and dream. I dream of trees standing like sentries. Standing to attention, silent. Heads shrouded in leaves and mist. The bark peels like flayed skin, revealing pale trunks, limbs. So many shades of green, so much smudged by the greying mind. I can feel their sopping leaves cloy around me. Cold water dripping down my hot neck. But ancestors stand beside the trees, their own skin dry and brown, like clay. Their faces strong, eyes dark. The road is slippery, slicked with oil, the white lines melt and spread, fat and slimy. The trees form a wall across the road and the bus veers and slides down into the forest gorge. Part of my soul slips and falls with the bus. My face smashes with the window. Glass cuts into my skin, embeds into bone. My eyes ... I can't see any more. My dark blood drains, leaving only the white. In the distance a siren wails.

But the trees line the road, closing it in, eating the dark clay under the bitumen, keeping the bus on its path. It was only a dream.

Calling Long Distance

I'm still looking out over the blue of the sea.

'Have you seen the island yet, Fab?' Nana asks from that long distance call.

'No, I haven't found it yet, Nana.'

'You will, my darling,' Nana reassures and the telephone squeals in protest as the money runs out.

'I'll call you when I find Ullagundahi,' I yell and the line drops out. Hang up and walk away. Go back to the bar and wait for the pub to fall from the edge of the world into the sea.

The Edge of the World

Looking over the edge of the world.

'Look further,' it calls. 'Deeper. Beyond the shallows. Go beyond the edge of this land. Come into the other world. Go on, immerse yourself,' it calls, teasing. 'Deeper, past the rip, the rock pools, the frothing waves. Beyond the layers of blue. Can you see them? They are not blue. They are grey. They are woy woy. They are Bundjalung. They are the ancestors. They are where you are from . . .'

Move that glass of beer over there and start writing . . . I just don't know what else to say, I think to myself. Who am I writing to anyway?

'Thought you might like a lemon squash,' he says.

'What do I want a lemon squash for?' Look up and in front of the pub, in front of the barman, in front of all the locals, we hug. I am crying. Around the bar they are shocked. It's not the done thing in Yamba. To cry in the pub.

'Honey, it's only lemon squash.'

'You followed the bus.' We sit down.

'You found it yet?' he asks.

I sip my remaining beer.

'Where you staying tonight?'

'Down past the lighthouse. The caravan park next to the river.'

'Wouldn't your rellies put you up?'

'Yeah, but you probably knew that, since you followed me.'

'Little Miss Independent, aren't you?'

But I'm looking out the window. He leans to me. Eye contact. 'What are you trying to prove? Who are you trying to prove it to?'

The barman comes over with a bowl of chips. He's threatening in a casual kind of way.

'You right, love?' he says as he puts down the bowl.

'Yeah, thanks. I'm fine. Do you have any prawn crackers?'

'No.' He frowns and walks back to the bar and says over his shoulder, 'We only got fresh ones round here.' Watch him walk back to the bar.

'Oops.'

'Talk to me. Don't you understand? I don't give a rat's backside who your family is.' He's leaning over the table again. He's looking for signs on my face.

'I need some fresh air.'

He salutes the watching barman with his beer and says to himself, 'Don't tell me. You ate the fish.'

All the drinkers hold on to their beers. They watch the sea with a new intensity.

It's beginning to get tricky here. I'm beginning to meander, like the river. I'm still looking. Watch me from the water . . .

As you drive towards the river country the air becomes warmer and there's a thawing within the soul. The trees, the green and the reflection of the sun on the water-laden land ease, calm. Wind down the windows as you drive along. Wave your arms in the warm currents of air.

He says, 'I understand why you always feel the cold down south now. I understand why you always need to be near the water. It's fantastic!'

But I'm thinking, I understand now the difference between a landscape that bakes, absorbs the sun into its very pores, and a land that uses water to mirror the light back into the sky, reflecting, refracting silver all around. I've found the wide blue-green Clarence. I have arrived home.

'Why would Nana leave such a beautiful landscape?' I ask the soft air and the warm light. 'Can we stop for a bit and have something to eat?'

'What, oh yeah, sure.' He pulls the kombi off the road and the tyres muck into the soft wet soil.

'Careful. The whole place has just been in flood. You'll sink the kombi.'

Stop the van. Immediately the soft buzz of insects fills our ears. The wind mingles with kombi fumes then washes them away. Sit and watch the river flow silently behind the reeds. I lean back and grab a bag out of the esky.

'Thought we were going to have some of those for dinner,' he says.

'Well, we can have some of them now, can't we?' I unwrap a white paper parcel on my lap and hand a boiled crab to him across the seat.

'Do you want one?'

He sighs. 'No. You go on.'

'Suit yourself then.' Break the claw with teeth. No need for tools.

'I'm going for a walk.'

'Well, be careful because the mud can be really deep.'

'Yeah, alright.'

He walks across the road to a wall of sugarcane. The debris from the recent flood lies sieved to the base of the grass. Sticks, branches, an old shoe. He picks up a large branch, bends it as if testing it for strength. He sighs, wonders when I'm going to see what he's looking at. He steps closer to the wall of sugarcane and breaks off a strand. It snaps cleanly. He pulls the sinewy leaves from it. The syrup begins to ooze slightly from the broken end. Droplets glisten in the sun. He walks back to car.

'Here. Got you a present.' He hands me the sugar over the crab shells. 'Did you eat them all?'

'Umm, I couldn't help it. I was really hungry. Oh, thanks.' Suck the sugar juice from the cane. 'It's chewy, isn't it? Here, have some.'

He climbs into the seat, starts the kombi. 'No thanks. So, did you eat *all* of the crabs?' Still chewing the cane I nod and choke, laughing.

'Four whole mud crabs?' He pulls the kombi back on the road.

'They were really fresh. You know seafood was a real luxury when I was a kid. You just couldn't get any. It would've been different for you.'

Potholes

I know we are heading into the 'Aboriginal' part of Casino as the straight bitumen road crumbles into tracks of dried mud. Potholes mark the beginning of the 'housing development'.

The Northern Rivers Aborigines have become fringe dwellers, their population decimated by massacre, their age-old culture, economy and way of life in ruins.

The fibro shacks seem to be pushed up by the tough grass that sprouts out of the foundations. The buildings do not stand straight, tall, but seem to waver and float above the green undulating hill. Some of the houses along the road have been painted, most have faded over the years to a pale mint. Old-style glass louvres break the monotony of the fibro walls. Over a few of them the odd jacaranda shelters the shacks from the sky.

'Aunty Mona, I've brought somebody to meet you.' She has a pale caramel face, the same colour as my Nana's, framed with short grey hair.

As I walk inside the fibro shack that is her home I can feel her studying the features of my face. She sits in her mauve dressing gown, holding her cup of tea.

She says, 'Hello?' at first questioning, then, 'Yes. Hello there,' as if she knows me, as if she has known me for a long time.

'Your face, I know . . . you're . . .'

'I'm Mabel Williams' granddaughter.'

'You're one of Nola's?'

'Yep. I've just travelled up—'

But a woman behind us in the doorway says, 'She came up to the community lookin' for her family. But there ain't no records.'

The marriage register of the Presbyterian Church shows many who were married at Ulgundahi . . .

1908: Jack Freeburn, of Yamba, married Mabel Davis (origin unknown, colour black)

'Oh, Mabel, yeah, she lived on the island till she got married,' says Aunty Mona. 'She was Jack Freeburn's granddaughter. She was named after her grandmother.'

'So, this one here, she's a Freeburn, yeah?'

'Yep, sit down, love, let's get you a cup of tea.' We sit down and pretended not to cry into our cups.

'You sit there, I've got some photos round here somewhere.' Aunty Mona forgets that she's only wearing her dressing gown and bustles around, searching, lifting piles of papers, folded sheets.

'Oh, I remember when Mabel lived on the island. She was an only child. Amy's. That's right. Very quiet as a girl. Shy. She lived in the "Freeburn" house with her grannies Jack and Mabel Davis . . . And how's your mother these days, she alright? What's she up to?'

Aunty's shack is small, the furniture old, vinyl covered. Neat, clean, worn out. She's looking around, fussing, and all the time she's asking me questions. We are discreetly dabbing our eyes.

'How's your sisters and where do you live? Is that mad mob still in Coober Pedy?'

She comes back from her linen cupboard with an old photo album. Its plastic cover is cracked and chipped with age.

'Here we go. I've got some photos here for you to look at.'

She opens the perishing album and starts pointing to faces. Black and white photos, newspaper cuttings, special events, babies, weddings.

There is photo of Nana.

She is a young girl with long dark hair swept back from her face, her forehead high. She is about ten or eleven, leaning against a paddock gate, a rough wooden structure crossing behind her. At her feet tufts of grass grow thick and strong. She is wearing a cotton dress, maybe a size too big for her, with a scooping neckline, short sleeves; the hem is loose, just below the knees. There is the same shy smile, although she's not looking at the camera. The sun is warm on her face, her skin is clear, smooth, and she is relaxed.

I bring my hand to my mouth with a gasp of shock. With this photo I realise so many things and I can't stop crying.

'Oh my Nana. She was so young.'

'It's alright.' Aunty Mona comes over and hugs my shoulders.

'She's so beautiful. She looks so young, so happy . . .'

'We all were once, you know. Life doesn't seem so bad when you're young. When you're young, nothing matters except warm weather and a good feed every now and then.' Aunty Mona sighs.

'Anyone want another cuppa?'

'Can I use your toilet?' Up come the crabs and the sugarcane and the tea.

We got rations . . . No aboriginal was allowed to go hungry . . . but it wasn't enough for us . . . we used to go hunting every day in the bush . . . A well-stocked store under the supervision of Mr Cameron on the island provided only the best brands of foodstuffs . . . Honey, porcupines, possum, goanna, kangaroo . . . We would chase them, throw stones at them and run them down, then take what we caught in the bush back to our Mum and Dad so we could have our meals.

'But why did she leave the island?'

'Well, she had to get work eventually, you know,' says Aunty Mona.

The children are taught in a school, the curriculum being adapted to the end of fitting them to earn a living the circumstances they are likely to experience. The girls, when old enough, are apprenticed at domestic work for five years at wages and under conditions laid down by the Government, and the money earned, after an allowance has been made to the worker for pocket money, is banked by the Board for the owner, whose interests are carefully watched in the spending of it.

'She went to Grafton and got work there. In one of the big houses.'

'She went to work for one of the big white families?'

'And then, well she met Lindsay and they fell in love.'

'Fell in love?'

'Yeah, you know, like how you young people fall in love these days. We weren't so different to you back then.'

'I know, I know, but . . . it's just she looks so young, happy . . .'

'When are you due, love?'

'Due?' I ask another question. 'Do you know which house she worked for?'

'No, couldn't say. They weren't really interested in us. We weren't really interested in them either . . .'

Domestic

I am reminded of a time when Nana was the local ironing lady. She did it to raise a bit of spare cash above and beyond her pension. A time, in Coober Pedy, when it could be forty plus outside and Nana would be standing at her ironing board, ironing, ironing. The rim of her enamel bowl the same blue as her varicose veins. All day long the iron would steam the damp cloth pressed over someone's uniform, someone's impossibly white shirt.

She became almost obsessed about ironing. I would wander down from the shower, holding my knickers to put them on away from the dust. She would grab them and say, 'Here, let me bump them over before you put them on.'

'But Nana, no one's gonna see.'

'Doesn't matter, it's nice to have pressed underwear.' And she would steam them under the iron, elastic and all . . . My memory evaporates with the steam.

And Aunty Mona says, 'We were just maids, ironing, washing, you know. She worked hard, your Nana. We all did.'

'But how come there are no records? There's nothing from on the island?' I ask.

'Well, Mabel wasn't born there, was she?' says Aunty Mona. 'No, Amy moved down south for a while. I think that had something to do with the old people, you know,' Aunty says quietly as she sips her tea. She doesn't look at me. I can hear the birds singing outside.

'You could ask at the Grafton Library, or the historical society . . . There's one in Grafton, or Maclean, somewhere. But they didn't do much on us blackfellas, you know.'

So I follow the potholes back to the bitumen. And the landscape changes, from propped-up shanty shacks to vast vibrant green plains, spotted with cows lining my nostrils with the acrid smell of fresh dung. Fragmented patches of forest bloom fade into suburban clusters where every house has a handkerchief of grass, neat, fenced and bordered with straight black roads. Within this single changing landscape there are two countries, divided neither by borders nor language, distance nor time.

There is a familiar hum of people reading, whispering, in the small, tidy room. Over in the corner decorated with streamers, balloons and primary-coloured egg cartons, kids scramble over beanbags and dog-eared books.

I smile. This could be anywhere in Australia. I rest my hands on the front counter and ask, 'Do you have any historical documentation on the local Aboriginal people that worked in the houses in the area.'

'I'm sorry, I don't know what you mean, really . . .'

'Oh, you know, things like sports teams, photos, fete days. Apparently there used to be big market days held down at the square.'

'The only written records we'd have about Aboriginal people would be if the well-to-do that kept diaries had mentioned their servants.'

'That would be unlikely though, wouldn't it?'

'Yes. People just didn't bother keeping records about the Aborigines in those days, unless, you know, it had something to do with the law, say if one was drunken and disorderly, or was dismissed for stealing, or something like that.'

Unfortunately, nature was kinder to us than the white people in Maclean, discrimination was very strong, i.e. roped off at the picture show, entrance through the dark side door, nasty remarks in the street as we passed by . . .

There is something in the way the librarian is saying this to me that makes me realise she is projecting her perceptions of what Aboriginal people are like today on the historical material she has.

I take a deep breath to confront her about what she is saying, for being nasty, racist. I look her straight in the eye. But I see in her face there is no malice. She is apologetic, almost sad about it.

'I'm looking for information about my Nana. I can give you her name, date of birth, where she lived, who she married.' I want to say all of this to the Grafton librarian.

I want to say, 'She described to me the jacarandas that grow along your main street—even though she hasn't been here for nearly twenty years.'

I am getting frustrated, angry. I'm getting sick of the words, 'Sorry, I can't help you, I'm afraid.'

In many ways, within and beyond Ullagundahi Island, Mabel Louise Freeburn simply did not exist.

Bridge

We walk over the Clarence River Bridge. It's a beautiful construction of iron studded with rivets. The pattern of triangles frames the town and fields around it.

We stand above the river. Looking down at the water flowing beneath us.

'So,' he says, leaning on the rail, 'what are we going to name him?'

'You knew?' I'm shocked and indignant.

'Oh yeah. I knew in Newcastle. When you got on the bus.'

'You've known all this time?'

'Yes.'

'Well, why didn't you tell me? Because I would've really liked to have known.'

'I was waiting for you to tell me yourself. It's your body!' He smiles and laughs. He puts his arm over my shoulders. 'Don't tell me you didn't know.'

'I thought it was the river, driving around. I thought it was the looking . . . I didn't think I could have babies. I'm the academic one. I'm not supposed to be having kids, you know. What the fuck are we going to do now?'

'Slowly slowly. Slowly slowly.'

I say, 'I am not swimming this river very well.'

'If it's a boy we'll call him Clarence,' he jokes. But I just cry harder.

'C'mon, honey. You're looking for your family tree—well, we're just growing our own branch.'

But I can't stop crying. He imagines tears dropping small and salty into the water below.

Norman Tindale

Norman Tindale has left a legacy that spans the entire continent. Norman Tindale was vicious in the detail of his work, his scientific rationale, his dedication to creating a nationwide Aboriginal genealogy.

Mr Tindale's Patience

In the matter of patience, however, they meet their match in Mr NB Tindale, the ethnologist at the Museum ... He spends hours on end with them, seated around a fire with a group as full of questions as the census taker ... Every native is allotted a number, and Mr Tindale's first task is to find out the name and the tribe of the subject; then whether he is married or single; whether he has children; if so, how many; whether they are males or females and similar queries. Of course, nearly all of this has to be done with an interpreter ... The native's memory is often short. Often questions seem to be evaded deliberately, but probably it is because the gist of them is not comprehended; but, with a wonderful display of patience, Mr Tindale repeats it in the same tone of voice half a dozen times, and usually gets some approach to satisfactory. Some of the subjects show comprehension of what is wanted, but others are heartbreakingly obtuse, and it is almost impossible to get anything from them ... His card filled in, the subject is passed on to the next section for examination. At the end of the line he receives a handful of sweets or raisins ...

Norman Tindale wrote about the Williams clan, mostly sired from 'Doctor Williams', a Bundjalung medicine man. Did the respected doctor of the Wodenbong community get a handful of sweets or sultanas? I do not know. What would 'Doctor Williams' have thought of these small pieces of sugar, of these shrivels of fruit? This man who could invoke the power of the Dreamtime with his hands. This man who created and sustained generations from his land. Norman Tindale's records, though fastidious, do not reveal the epic within each life, only the outlines of each birth–death link. He did not and could not touch the stories, the hopes, dreams and failures that kept Aboriginal people together, that made the family. Such scientific notes as 'deceased boy, age seven' are scribbled in the margins. He did not touch on how illness, disease, the squalor of living conditions, caused heartbreak. He did not see, or note, how hard these people worked to survive after being pushed from their lands and given meagre rations. That was too unscientific.

Doctor Williams' great-grandson, Gordon Williams, married Eva McBride late in life, according to Norman Tindale's records, but they had five children nonetheless. Anybody under the age of fifteen rarely rates a naming, just a gender and the shade of 'darkness'. Any exceptionally pale people were noted with a double asterisk.

When Norman Tindale breezed through Wodenbong

Mission, Gordon's son, Lindsay Williams, existed only as a male symbol next to three others and one female.

It is only through his parents' names and Nana's memories of him that I can trace him as my grandfather. When I find him and the genealogy reaching far back, I weep with a longing, a sighing of relief that I belong.

'Are you alright?' the woman who has found my genealogy asks.

I'm thinking about babies. I'm thinking about a new generation. Who's the youngest of our family? I am floundering, failing this search. Finding documents, papers about my family, about my Nana's life before I knew her. This is too haphazard, accidental.

I nod, crying. 'I'm happy. I'm just happy . . .'

'These things can be a bit emotional at times.' The woman pats my hand and leaves me to it.

Sultanas and scribbles trace the bloodline. At the top of the genealogy Tindale has written, 'Fb1, male. Fb2, female. The banks of the Clarence River.'

'Fb' means full blood.

Lindsay Gordon Williams

Although the scribble is static, forever sealed, unnamed, ink on paper, hidden, stored, it did not stop Lindsay Gordon Williams from living his own life.

Static documents, assimilation policies, mission censuses did not stop Lindsay falling in love with Mabel Louise Freeburn. Her beautiful dark brown eyes, her dark brown hair. How could you not love someone like that? The way she looked when she smiled, that dimple, it would send you just about crazy.

'We thought we loved each other,' said my Nana once, almost to herself. 'But we were too young. And they just wouldn't leave us alone.'

'Who wouldn't, Nana?'

'Oh, the old people, our families. Everybody had to put in their two cents' worth,' she sighed.

'His family didn't think I was good enough for him. I was too white, too lah-di-dah.' Looking into the distance. 'So what did we do? We got married, that's what. Bloody stupid idiots . . . but that's what happened.'

And Aunty Mona is telling me back in her fibro shack, 'That's your cousins there, and I'm your aunty cause I married your grandfather's brother. And your Nana, she moved off the island, married Lindsay Williams and came and lived here in Casino.'

'They lived here?'

'Yeah, just up the road a bit. We were neighbours for ages.

'Look here, that's their wedding.' She slides the album towards me. There is my Nana, standing, her long black hair swept back and tucked in the typical 1940s fashion. She holds a trailing bouquet of flowers and she wears a long white gown with a heart-shaped neckline and mutton-legged sleeves. The fabric flows long and sweeps down to the floor; she stands tall and smiles demurely.

Framed by the veil, she radiates shy happiness. Mabel is twenty-one.

The marriage certificate reads:

That on the 24th of August, 1944, Lindsay Gordon Williams married Mabel Louise Freeburn at St Mary's Church, Casino, according to the rites of the Church of England.

The marriage is witnessed by Lindsay's father, Gordon Williams, and mother, Eva McBride, and Mabel's mother, Amy Freeburn.

'She was a stunner that day. No expense was spared. Her mother and aunty slaved for that gown. She got what she wanted.'

'What happened to the dress, Aunty Mona?'

In other photos she stands alone.

'What happened to it? It's a mystery, no one knows. It just disappeared. I would've given anything to have a wedding dress like that,' wishes Aunty Mona.

'If only they'd just left us alone,' sighed Nana.

It almost seems to me that with the changing of Nana's last name came seven children from some mythical creature, a Grandpa Williams.

Lindsay Williams' 'usual occupation' was with the AIF and it was a running joke within the family that every time his personnel card had 'AWOL' stamped on it, Mabel fell pregnant.

Seven times. Once with twins. Uncle Peter, Uncle Paul. Once with triplets. Miscarried. Unspoken of. Unnamed. Mabel had a heart attack for every child she carried.

Lindsay Williams grins but his eyes are looking beyond the camera, at Mabel maybe. His dark curly hair is slicked back under his slouch hat. One eyebrow is raised. He is very handsome, high cheekbones, high forehead; he looks rugged, healthy and distinctive. Very swish. You can see why Mabel fancied him.

Lindsay Williams was a typical Australian soldier, cheeky and full of life in his uniform, except his skin was the deep colour of clay.

The AIF went to war, young men, young Aboriginal men . . . Egypt, Papua New Guinea . . .

So many casualties he witnessed, so many of his friends died in front of him, guts exploding, land mines ripping off limbs, corpses hanging like Christmas baubles from barbed wire. Hadn't he already survived a war? Hadn't his family seen enough blood? He didn't want this for his life. He came back from these battles bloodied, changed. Touched.

Lindsay Williams returned but was not recognised as a soldier by the Australian government because he was Aboriginal. He took to the bottle in madness and for comfort . . .

So many casualties. Sanity being one.

When the sun set on those summer days in Casino the shadows in the bushes became the enemy. Gotta protect the kids, gotta protect the missus. 'Quick, come inside, kids! I don't care if it's hot. Get inside now!' Explosions went off in Lindsay's head.

'Shh, for Christ's sake shut up, you lot. Do you want your heads shot off? Keep down. Keep away from the windows.' Shrapnel sung past him in all directions, miraculously missing the kids. 'Shut up now!' He back-handed one against the table.

'Get down! I'm going out. Wait here until I give the all-clear.'

He thought he was doing right by his wife. He was only doing it to protect his kids. Protect his country.

'When Lindsay was sober he was a good man. When he drank he was like the devil himself.'

'He used to belt Mum,' one of my uncles once told me. Then his lips sealed and he looked away.

Eventually Mabel fled from her husband, from her river, from her country.

I imagine the wedding gown thrown from the banks of the river. I see it luminous in the setting sun. Floating, the shiny soft flowing fabric muddying with the river's waters, slowly soaking, submerging. I see the long pale veil trailing behind along the surface. Floating with the current of the river, softly, slowly. Floating out to sea.

Mabel left her land behind and followed her mother to Tennant Creek. She took her children to her mum. Like a peace offering. There was no one to see her off.

At Tennant Creek she found red sand, and new love.

I Found my Thrill on Blueberry Hill

When Bruno looked into Mabel's deep brown eyes gazing adoringly up at him that night on Blueberry Hill, he lied to her. They held on to each other in the front seat of Bruno's blue ute, overlooking the sleeping town.

'Bruno?'

'Hmmm?'

'When is your birthday? I want to buy you a present.' Bruno had to think fast. He did not want Mabel, with seven children in her saddlebags, to spend her scrubbing money on him.

'I'm a leap year baby,' he said, his blue eyes twinkling. 'Twenty-ninth of February.'

Mabel sighed and rested her head on Bruno's shoulder. They watched the moon rise like a golden balloon into the blue-black sky. The town of Tennant Creek took on a luminous glow and slowly house lights blinked out. A hush had descended. Streets were deserted, save for the lone wanderer or stray mongrel searching for scraps. The day's red dust settled and the town seemed to be wrapped in a purple haze. From a distant ute, glowing in the moonlight, country music tinkled softly.

On her dressing table, covered with dust from the dugout wall, Nana had many bottles of perfume. As girls Sandra and I would flick back the curtain that was the door to Nana's bedroom, jump up to switch on the light hanging from the ceiling. Then we would tiptoe up to Nana's dresser. None of the perfume had been used. Nana didn't wear perfume. I would look at these little ornaments and wonder if Bruno gave them to her. Bottles the shape of butterflies with gold stoppers as their heads. Or flowers, or the shape of old-fashioned ball dressers. Bottles with names like Romance, Joy and Jonquil Kiss. Bright golden fluid that over the years had just evaporated into the air, into the dust. We were allowed to open and smell them. But they stank of sweet baby sick or sticky hair spray, of cheap brandy mixed with Jasol or Pine O Cleen. Us kids preferred the smell of frying pork chops or pumpkin scones. We would doodle tracks in the dust that had settled on the lacquered surface, then leave the bottles untouched. I wondered how long it took for Bruno to realise Nana didn't wear perfume.

But she couldn't throw anything away. She would keep everything. Not only bottles of unused perfume but jewellery she rarely wore, cupboards full of old cards. Birthday cards, school reports, scraps of material kept to make unfinished quilts, newspaper cuttings featuring her children, funeral cards from Aunty Ag's passing. Ribbons from baby booties. The plastic baby bath she washed me in on the kitchen table, so old the colour had faded around its edges. Plastic flowers, dried wild flowers, favourite editions of *Women's Weekly*. Suitcases of old clothes.

I found a photo of Bruno and Nana taken when they still lived in Tennant Creek. It is a black and white photo, with an old white border around its edges. The details are clear enough. They are at a hall, sitting around a table covered in glasses. In the background others are also seated, drinking, or dancing. Bruno's dark hair is slicked back and he wears a crisp shirt. He leans into Nana. She is sitting beside him and her head is tilted towards his, smiling, almost embarrassed. Bruno is looking at her and his eyes are bold, almost devastating. He is confident, relaxed. Her hand is placed next to his, not touching, but close.

This is not my Nana. This is Mabel and Bruno. Still young and undeniably in love. The chemistry between them is unmistakable, almost startling. She would follow him when he got opal fever. He would build her a dugout. He would concrete over the hill that threatened to erode her bedroom. They would wake each other up with their snoring.

During the years that followed Bruno would ask, 'Okay, you kids, where's my present?'

'But it's the twenty-eighth, Bruno,' the kids would whine.

'Huh,' he would grumble, all the time his face cracking with a grin.

Later, many years later, when the dust of Coober Pedy had cracked open the skin of Bruno's fingers, had wedged under his nails and forced them from the skin:

Dearest Fab
Bruno went into hospital again yesterday and should be out tonight or tomorrow. He went in last week and he had injections in his fingers and his toes. He said it didn't hurt much but it made me feel sick to see his poor fingers and toes like that . . .

When the dust of time had settled on and faded Bruno's face, Nola, looking to update his hospital records, found his passport from Italy.

His date of birth: 3 October.

'Why didn't you tell Mum, Bruno?'

'I didn't want her buying presents for me *every* year,' he smirked, triumphant.

Ullagundahi Island

After Aunty Mona's we drive back to Yamba and stand on the top of the cliff. I look out to the sea for answers. It seems the more answers I seek the more questions I have to ask. We walk down from the cliff, saluting the white penis–lighthouse as we pass. We climb down onto the beach and trace the blue sea back along the coastline into the murky green-blue of the river.

The sun has begun to set and the wind heralds in new clouds to muddy the sky.

'Everything is so wet and soggy. Even the ground.' I push my feet into the soil. We walk alongside the river. The salty water churns with the fresh and eats away the land.

'Everything smells. Can you smell it? Sort of like bread mould, but greener.' The wind has picked up and the waves work harder to form more foam.

'Yeah, but the sea air, it's so fresh and salty. Like fish,' he says.

'On one side the sea. On one side the river. On both sides the fish. And everywhere—' I shout into the wind '—the water!'

'And fish,' he grins.

'Oh yeah, fish. I feel like I'm on the Manly Ferry again.' I hold his arm to steady myself.

'If you're going to chuck up, do it in the water. Feed those that have been feeding you.'

'You're such a greenie sometimes.' I lie down on the grass. The ground squishes beneath. Looking up at the darkening sky I can feel the water seeping into my clothes, wetting my skin.

'Only one more place to go,' I say to the clouds above.

He comes up and yanks me from the ground.

'Wait till tomorrow.'

'Can we stay at the pub tonight? I can't hack camping any more.'

'Yeah, alright.'

Rocky Laurie

At the caravan park office a woman in her late forties sits behind the laminated desk. Seeing us come in, she turns down her mini television.

'G'day, love, what can I do for ya?'

'Um, I was wondering if I could move from the camping site to a cabin tonight?'

'The rain's nonstop this time of the year.'

'Yeah, the tent was pretty damp last night.'

'They say the river might flood.'

'Again?'

'Well, you never know in this part of the world, love. How long ya staying for?'

The descendants of the original tribes who still live at Yamba are housed at Pippi Beach in homes built in 1962. The road leading out there is called Rocky Laurie Drive in honour of an aborigine who achieved a great reputation as an all-round sportsman on the Lower Clarence.

'Oh, a while . . . Umm . . . I was wondering . . .'

'Yes, love?' The caravan woman looks up briefly from the television.

'Do you know where Rocky Laurie Drive is?'

'Rocky Laurie? No . . . no . . . can't say I do.'

'Well, it's just that it's supposed to be around here somewhere, it goes out to the local Aboriginal community?'

'Aboriginal community? Stan! Do you know whether there's an Aboriginal community round here? I must say, love, I've lived here for ten years and I've never heard of an Aboriginal community close by . . . You sure you don't mean Maclean, or somewhere like that?'

'No, apparently there's a road out of Yamba, Rocky Laurie Drive . . .'

Stan comes in. 'Yeah, whadya want? Oh.' He sees me.

He once competed in the Stawell Gift . . .

'Try driving south along the coast. There are a few houses down that way. They're pretty run-down.'

. . . but lack of racing experience under such conditions went against him . . .

'Don't know if anybody lives in them any more,' he says. Eyes drift to the television.

Along the outskirts of town the coastal wind blows the sand over Rocky Laurie Drive. Beyond the bush-studded dunes waves rip the blue-green water and crash onto the beach. The sea-immense is hungry and eats away at the land. Huddled away from the dunes and off the road a small group of buildings form a circle. I walk towards the buildings and the dark-clay coloured people within them. I don't know them and they don't know me but I can't stop smiling, and if I don't keep check of myself I'll start crying for no reason.

'G'day, love. Where you from, girlie? Which family you from?'

'Yeah, we know where Ullugandahi is, of course we do. Half this mob's from there. You just follow the river back inland from the sea.

'Keep goin' inland, head for the mountains, follow the road. Don't worry 'bout the big islands. Ullagundahi's only a little one. You can't miss it. You just follow the river.'

'Where's your Nana, is she with you? Well, we'd come with you, love, we would, but there's a funeral, an old fella, diabetes, you know . . . Let us know how you go.

'Call out, someone will come over with a boat.'

The island has been used as an aboriginal station since about the year 1908 . . . Fittingly it is situated on a spot in the river in sight of Ashby, on the mainland where the tribes from up and down the Clarence River in the heyday of the aborigines used to gather . . .

The kombi bogs in the clay-coloured mud so I step out and walk through the forest to get to river.

Trees try to descend like a wall of water. Sea green. Yet seemingly suspended in time by the fence that divides the forest from the field, the soil from the plough. Sea green with a hint of yellow, a touch of amber smoke in the cold air. The trunks deep brown, thin, straight and sombre—all reaching, racing against each other for the first drops of rain, the first warmth of the sun. Each tree has its own shape, its own shading and colour, its own way of pushing up into the canopy. If trees were human it would seem that these were stretching out their arms, throwing out their hands in the sheer glory of life.

'You can't miss it. It's right opposite Grafton—you can see it from the banks of the river,' Nana said.

An island of blood clotted in Nana's brain. It caused her stroke. It confused her. The memories of her childhood have faded. The landscape of her youth has changed.

I know because I'm standing on the banks of the

Clarence looking out across the water, muddied green-brown in the wake of the recent floods. The water has washed down from the mountains and fills the streets of Grafton and Maclean with mud. Majestic stone houses and fibro shacks alike sit in the lowlands, some wallowing under metres of water. The people can do nothing except move to the hills, the mountains. Surrounding cane fields are waterlogged, the bright green leaves trapping the water to the land. Sodden. The light of the landscape is subdued, tinted with a clouded grey-green. Everyone waits for the land to drain itself, to push the water from its soil, back into the flowing river, back out to sea.

'Hello! Is anybody there?' The force of my voice pushes my feet deeper into the mud. It echoes off the water and bounces back. 'Hello, hello.' The island is mocking, distant.

The grey-green of the trees and the bright, almost brittle green of the cane fields camouflage and sculpt the island into the opposite bank. It's as if it doesn't exist.

I'm am so close but I can't get across. Should I swim? Upstream debris floats hurriedly by. This river is alive. I can't leave now I've found it. Everything smells wet, pungent. Every now and then the sun breaks through the uncommon clouds and the water flashes silvery light. Wince and blink. Momentarily blinded.

I yell out again. 'Cooo-eee! Is anybody there? Hello!'

From out of the cane fields comes a dark man. His hair is black and he wears big, bright blue gumboots. He wades towards the edge of the island and squints into the sun.

'Hello! I've come to visit the island. Can I come across?' I wave frantically. He turns and walks back into the cane.

Looking at the river again, I can see the current rippling the water. I'm a pretty strong swimmer.

I look around for somewhere to keep my clothes dry but everything is wet. It feels as though the land is like a sponge, saturated. My trousers are muddied and stained to the knees. I take a step towards the river and my shoes are sucked into the mud. I'm trying not to slip. Standing on one leg the slight movement of colour draws my attention to the men in a dinghy crossing the river towards me. They cut through the moving water like a knife sculpting soft, pale clay.

I'm relieved and embarrassed. I wave. I'm still standing on one leg.

The dinghy arrives.

'Hello.' Again. I'm looking down and groping for my shoe in the soup I'm standing in.

The men stand shyly on the banked dinghy, looking at me quizzically as I try to explain.

'I couldn't keep away . . .'

Then after a time, 'It's bloody wet around here, isn't it?'

They nod, chuckling.

'Flood,' says one. His frog-like smirk reminds me of someone I know.

Together, quietly, awkwardly, we return to the island.

I step off the dinghy, climb up the mud and walk to the flat open field next to the cane.

'Where have all the houses gone?'

'Washed away in the flood.'

'You mean last week?'

'No, back in '45.'

The 1921 flood had been a bad experience but the next did not occur until 1928 and after that there was a break until 1945. It was hazardous for the residents and their rescuers to be taken off the island. After the sequence of floods from 1945–54, and a big one in 1963, the decision was taken to provide housing on the mainland.

'Well, where were all the houses before?'

'Oh, they were all over the place, this empty part here, see?' He points to the open area of land. It is like a large shallow basin, dotted with the odd rotten wood post. Grass grows roughly, haphazardly, swathes of it flattened in the mud. On the far edge of the basin a lone rose bush grows, its leaves tinged red. There are no flowers on it, no blossoms, it struggles and fights the grass slowly choking it. I'm walking towards it, asking the men, 'Where was the Freeburn house?'

One of the men waves his arm around vaguely. 'Oh,

round here some place. Most of the houses were fairly close together.'

'There was one down that end of the island, near the edge.'

He points to the dark blue-green mountains brooding in the distance.

'But it got washed away.'

'They all did, or they just rotted and fell apart.'

'No one here to look after them, see.'

'And when the school went . . .'

'Went where?'

'Washed down the river.' The man points. 'Went out to sea, all smashed up, it did,' he says.

I nod, looking around, trying to imagine the houses huddled together on the island. Feet are numb, cold, sodden. Overhead, the clouds bunch closer together and cast the island in a shadow of grey.

And, instead of being cooped up between the brick and concrete walls of a town, forced to wear uncomfortable clothes and compete with the white men in social graces to hold their position in the ranks of the toilers, they live under a wide sky, surrounded by the great arms of a noble river, on an island set in a glorious valley, where the flowering trees and shrubs grow all about their doors, their children paddle their boats on the surface of the river in the glow of the sunset and no white man or woman may land in their little island without the permission of the man whose job in life it is to make things as easy for them as he can with the resources of the government at his back.

I feel a strange sensation that the island is sinking. The surrounding river is murky with mud scraped from the streets of the towns. It churns and sifts the island through its water. On the surface the river is calm, but feel the current eating away Ullagundahi. I realise the current would be too violent for those not strong enough.

I needed to come, to find out who I am. I needed to walk on this island. This beautiful green Ullagundahi. But I see Nana now. I see her as a young half-caste girl going to the school with her relatives.

I see Grandpa Freeburn's island. It is not a sanctuary, it is where they put them, it is a prison, in the margins, on the fringes. They put these people on fragments of land suspended by water. Refugee camps in the middle of the river. Refugee camps for those dispossessed. Are we dispossessed? Who really belongs here?

The Isle of the Vanishing Men
Stone Age to Twentieth Century
Ulagunadahi Settlement Makes People Happy
Laughter and Song, Work, Flowers and a Protector Cares for the Conquered Race . . .

Are we a conquered race? Should I keep reading these old papers I've found?

No. I should just listen to the dolphins. I should talk to the people.

I see Mabel Louise Freeburn as a young woman, working as an anonymous domestic over in Grafton. I see her as a mother, struggling, working to bring up her kids. I don't know the details, the heartbreak she must have felt seeing her husband ignored and rejected by his country. The country he fought for. How strange a country that acknowledges only one side of history, one side of war. Nana's life must have been hard, but after all this work, all this time, there is no anger in Nana, only acceptance and self-belief, a self-preservation so strong it could only have come from a culture of survivors. I look over this green, lush landscape, full of water and life. Full of promise.

'Well, then everybody moved onto the mainland,' says one of the men standing beside me.

I see a pink tinge of blood flowing through this river of dolphins. It seeps from the soil into the water and out over the edge of the world. With it seeps my Nana's youth.

No dolphins swim past as we cross back over the Clarence. I step onto the mainland, and the man with the smirk says, 'You know, I'm probably related to you.'

'Yeah, I know.' I smile and wave goodbye.

At least now I have found Ullagundahi. I have walked on the island and I can tell Nana that I have uncovered what I was looking for.

Awake Time

At the edge of the world the sun has set and outside the window at the Yamba pub it is black. No one's fishing tonight. Storm coming. Wait for the fish to come up the river. The pub's full. It's a night off, a night of drinking. A night for avoiding the mistress sea. But even the locals can't ignore the clouds blotting the stars from the window. There are no curtains. There is no need for them on a cliff. The edge of the world has turned black.

'You can stop looking now,' he says. 'There's nothing to see.' I turn to him.

'Yeah, you're right. What are you having?'

'I thought just a veggie stir-fry.'

'Oh, yep. Okay. You want me to order?'

'No, you sit. So, you want the seafood cocktail, the fisherman's basket and the prawn salad?'

'Yep.' Smile.

'Fuck.' He sighs, but doesn't get up to order. Drink for a while.

'When are we going home, honey?' he asks.

Silence. I'm not wanting to talk.

'Alright. When are you going to tell your family?'

'When I'm ready.'

'You can't hide it forever.'

'I'm not hiding. I'm waiting.' I get up to order. 'I'm really hungry.'

'When are you going to tell your Nana?'

'You want me to know when is the right time?' I ask.
'I want to tell her in person In my own way.'

Time

I wait for the right moment to call her. I wait for a sign
from the sky, the river, the light, flashing from the
water, but nothing happens. For three days I wait. I look
to the landscape. I stop reading those books. I know
who I am now. I stay awake and look to the river, to the
edge of the world, the sea and into my beer. I wait and
after three days of dreaming, I fall asleep.

I wake up to the ringing of a phone in a distant room.

And how do I wake up? With an opening of my eyes.

Blink blink. It is still dark. I'm in this hotel bedroom.
High above ground, above dirt, above rock. High above
the sea. All I see is black, but if I keep my eyes open for
a while the light seeps through. Pale, powdery. Beside
me he softly snores.

The phone is still ringing. I answer it.

After that Nana's life blots out. It's an emptiness.
A blackness. A wall of trees, sucking all energy, all
queries, all questions. Only silence.

Blink blink and I am back in Coober Pedy. But I am
no longer a child, floating in the soft dust of my
dreaming. I am awake.

Funeral Notice

The FUNERAL of the
late Mrs Mabel WILLIAMS
who died on 10/7/94
will be held on THURSDAY 14th JULY, 1994
at 10.00 am
departing from the
COOBER PEDY HOSPITAL
to the COOBER PEDY CEMETERY
where a grave-side service
will be held.

• • •

Stuck on the glass door, in the front of Lucases, one of only two supermarkets in this one pub town, Cooher Pedy. I walk past it, turn around, staring, realising who it belongs to. The sticky tape is peeling, yellow and perishing from the dust on the glass. The paper glowing gold from the orange sunset flowing through the door. The edges of the paper ragged. The warmth from the sun touches my face, dust particles float on the golden air, touching everything, leaving a film of dust everywhere, all over my body, not to be removed until I wash myself back in Adelaide, but by then the dust has seeped into my pores, settled into every crevice, sunk through the layers of skin and become part of my blood. I let it sink into me while staring at the glass, at the notice, realising that it's about my Nana, about someone I know, someone who shopped here at this hick-town half-empty super-market at least three times a week for twenty-three years of her life.

She used to come in the back way, down the hill from the front door of her dugout. Everybody knew her, so it didn't matter. It was all part of the ritual.

Except on Thursdays. On Thursdays the truck would come in and block her way. Packers would be frantically ripping open boxes, finding invoices stuck in obscure places, trying to restock the empty shelves before the hoards came in, demanding more. Wanting to know where the Jarlsberg cheese was, the fresh olives, the vacuum-sealed bacon, the rare and very expensive fish.

I worked as a packer occasionally, with my mother and aunt, hating every moment. The smells, the ripping of the fingernails on the cardboard. Cold fingers, standing in the fridge, restocking, repacking while impatient customers stood behind me demanding new stock.

'Get me the vanilla custard. No, the big one, at the back. Here, get out the way, I'll get it myself.'

I used to think, 'How undignified, how demeaning, how unsophisticated,' wanting to be back in Adelaide. But now I realise dignity comes from the mind, not from the location. And I only hated the work because I wasn't very good at it.

On Thursday Nana would come through the front of Lucases. Through these very doors, and even before then, when these doors weren't glass but roller doors, and this place a tin shed.

I stare at the notice. I stand for a moment, remembering.

The funeral has passed . . .

The priest reads about a woman unknown to him, as Father Paul, a long-time friend of the family, has left. We say 'friend' only, as we are not a religious family. We are not churchgoers and neither was Nana. Who needs to go to church when you have faith and humour in life at home? Father Paul understood Nana, he understood all of us. He once talked my sister Sandra out of Catholicism, as a favour to Mum. But he's not here by the grave. 'God' has sent him away from Coober Pedy, from his home for so many years. This new priest knows that he has a long haul before he's considered a 'local' and he bears his alienation with dignity. He reads . . .

The service rambles on. Through the tears, the gut-wrenching sobs, there is something within me, standing apart, not really believing, looking at the sun, the blue sky, searching for her spirit and thinking, 'These words mean nothing. They say nothing about her, her soul, her life. Isn't this what any family would say about their grandmother, their matriarch?'

But these words are all we could think of. Our brains are numbed with shock and grief—it's all we could say, all we could share. We are not of the great poets.

Around the grave we are all trying to be on our best behaviour, yet our characteristics and personalities are strongest while we are trying to be what Nana would've wanted. Our frailties and our faults are solidified. Even the sunlight and the tears can do nothing to burn out the fact that no matter how different we all are, or how similar, we are a family who has lost someone we love—love being a word that does nothing to explain the depth and magnitude of our feelings.

Orchids, roses, native hops, carnations, lilies,

banksias, proteas, daisies, she loved them all. We smother her in flowers.

Her body is now the soil, the red earth, encrusted with the blood of life. My hands embrace the dust that embraces her. I push my hair from my face absent-mindedly. The dust, red, remains and stains me with the smell of the desert, of the land, of Nana and her dugout and memories of a life I only really half knew.

And now I'm standing in the front of Lucases, the sun streaming on my face with the defiance that is raised after a loss, like the way we Australians are so ridiculously proud of Gallipoli.

She is laid to rest now; everybody that needs to know, knows. I tear off the notice, hoping to capture the gold of the sunset in the paper, hoping to capture the dust settling on me, the moment itself.

Later my uncle finds the notice between my magazines, stored and hidden from any embarrassment. He had put the notice up, being the dutiful son, trying to keep as busy as possible while working with his own grief. He looks at the notice, at me, but says nothing.

The dying sunlight now streams through the doorway, unhindered, slowly turning red. The sun is in my eyes, but I do not blink, I do not close my eyes, I let it burn into me, burn into my very retinas. People pass at the edge of my vision. I turn to do the shopping, knowing there's no need to look for her in the dusty aisles, she's not here. She's in the glow of the sunset and the dust that is on my skin and in my blood.

Memories

Sometimes I capture a whiff of Johnson & Johnson talcum powder. Breathe it in. Hold on to it. I never use it. Haven't since I left Coober Pedy. It doesn't smell right on me. It smelt so good on Nana. Nostalgia. That is what it smells like. In the end memories are old but alive like pain, like blood.

It never stops flowing.

5. Flow

My Ashlyn May

It is so peaceful here before the storm of the day. The weather has a calm about it soothing to the skin. The clouds look like streaks of ink in the sky, bleeding softly down into the sea. Today is a day to calm the panic within. I feel like the fat red boulder sitting in the eye of a dust storm. The trees act as tranquil solace, as sentries, holding my sanity. I'm waiting for the sun to crack me open. How did the mothers of my family survive this so many times?

Since Nana has gone I miss my mum so intensely, though I believe we don't really know each other beyond the telephone. And I feel I haven't spent any great deal of time with her since I left home ten years ago. Ever since then it's been captured moments of conversation slotted between the rest of our lives.

Reports. And when I do see her, face to face, in the same town or city, we seem to avoid each other and busy ourselves with inconsequentials, like shopping or television.

It's like she knows me by form (I am from her body after all) but not by colour. A grainy photograph of a painting. From a distance. I wonder if we are simply too intense for each other. Too different. Too similar. We are linked by blood. Perhaps that should be enough. That's where the crux of my confusion lies. Most times I am relieved at the distance between us. It gives me the space to be cathartic, to be myself when the mood grips (and it gets me often). There are other times when I look around, searching for her, waiting for her to come through the door and pick up the conversation we've just left off. It's only when she doesn't appear that I realise the conversation has taken place inside my head. A lifelong dialogue, our telephone calls merely its footnotes. The ritual of phoning, the physical process before I hear her voice and can ascertain if it's okay to talk now, makes it so. Just a brief note, a call to let her know . . . what? Something, anything so long as it's newsworthy. It has to justify the phone call itself. The act of phoning. The money. It means that there is nothing inconsequential about our conversations, about our relationship. Every word has its impact. We've been throwing words at each other for years now. Distance makes it so. I just wonder what it would be like if she lived here. Would the tumble of words stop, slow, cease? Would we assume more, living in each other's landscape, each other's painting? I just wonder. And I wonder why I'm asking this now.

Wait

I am about to have a daughter. I think it's a daughter. A little girl. My 'little ray of sunshine'. My uncles used to sing that song to each other. At least I hope it's a daughter. The ultrasound guessed at a daughter. Hope and pray and wait. Very strange things for me to do. I like to worry, to act, to rant, wave my arms about and demand. And slam doors. I am not patient, nor reasonable. I am never rational or calm. I cannot submit myself to fate. At least not without question. I remain very angry at God, and when I feel righteous, the idea of God. Melodrama has always been my middle name. My undoing. Those that know me accept my scars as part of me, like a mark I cannot wash from my face. Those that don't do best to avoid me.

Patience

To hope and pray. These require much too much patience on my behalf. Too much tolerance. These things are entirely out of my character. Did I inherit this from Mum? I don't think so. To me she has always met adversity with a cheerful bloody-mindedness. If the situation was beyond humour, she always got the job done. I used to scowl with hatred at the way she would do this, deal with her life. Looking back I was far too precocious to be her child. I remember screaming, 'I HATE YOU!' as she drove past us in Bruno's blue ute one time. She was only going up the hill to Nana's dugout. Nana said she could hear me from her doorstep. I remember trying to call her 'idiot' like the Greek boys mocking their mothers up at the school. A slap across the face taught me that wouldn't work. I still feel embarrassed about that. Is this youth, the insolence of childhood? Wonder what I'm going to do when my child tries that on me.

Fear and Procrastination

From your brothers and sister I get the message that you were always the practical, bossy one, Mum. Pragmatic. Did you adopt this policy of practicality when I came into your life? Will motherhood make me so? It is something I fear within myself.

I already feel far too practical to be creative. Unbalanced by domesticity. Can I be eccentric as a mother without endangering my baby? Is this why I am looking, searching for my history? I'm frightened of being trapped in pink and blue Tupperware. I'm beginning to ignore the dishes and hide within my writing again. My whole body is settling like mud in water. I can't see what I was afraid of any more. But I've always needed something to hide from in order to get anything else done in my life.

Perhaps I'm seeking an overload. But that's when the physical breakdown begins. An overload is going to happen when the baby comes anyway. I'm hiding in my storytelling again, aren't I? I'm trying to hide from the possible pain of birth and responsibility. It's why I'm writing and why I don't want to stop working. But now I realise I need the energy anyway.

Sugar Addiction

Work, write and gestate. I think I can't do it all. Not without props, cajoling and promising. I am the proverbial pregnant donkey. I need the carrot on the stick to keep me going. Sweet treats. Pamper me or I will sulk. Sugar addiction. It's my lifelong habit. But Mum never indulged me and I wonder where it comes from, this lax will, this habit of unconditional spoiling I insist from those around me. I'm so weak and she is so strong. She had three of us. Three daughters. Endured the humiliation of a hospital system that I now scream about. I know she wasn't passive because she was angry about it and in that she was strong. She went in, had her babes and walked out. The hospital where I was born is being redeveloped into yuppie apartments. At first I was outraged as the advertising banner yelled 'It's happening!' to all who drove past. Such bloody irony. Then I consoled myself with the thought that at least the building wasn't knocked down and thousands of people can still pass and say, 'Hey, that's where I was born.' But I can't believe that the memories of labouring women and newborn children will not seep through the fashionable new paint. 'It's happening!' Ha. Sounds like the beginning of contractions.

Endure

It was something to endure for so many generations. I refuse to believe it's the same during mine. Even when they say to endure is for the benefit of the baby. When the hospital tells me to endure humiliation for the benefit of the baby, they imply it's my selfishness and irrational pride questioning what is best. But to seek information is my right as an unbirthed mother, isn't it?

What would you say, Mum? Why can't I just pick up the phone and ask you?

The fabric of this dress rides up and curls under my

swollen belly, as if opening me up for the birth. Sweat drips under my arms, pools between swollen breasts. I'm angry at the heat, at the weight. I've been categorised as having gestational diabetes. They say the heat and fluid could be caused by that. As if pregnancy is not reason enough.

They think it's my Aboriginal 'genetic heritage' that makes my body sensitive to sugar. It's the generations before me that mark me apart in the system. It's the blackness of my blood. But what about my European heritage? What about Dad's side of the family? The Belgians are famous for their chocolates, thick, sweet and creamy. Images of sugared waffles come to mind. Hot chips and rich egg mayonnaise. In Brussels stalls sell this richness to a history of people, thickening their blood, clogging the streets and arteries. Did I inherit my sweet tooth from my Belgian nana along with her gnarled toes and disposition to hypochondria? If so, then my body has been booby-trapped by my ancestors. I wonder what I will pass on to my child. If only we could pick out our best features for our children, like favourite clothes from the dresser. If that was the case, pregnancy wouldn't be such a loaded state and I wouldn't be so weighed down with love and patience. I would break off these shackles with hysteria. I'd be more spontaneous and creative. I'd indulge my sugar habit and eccentricities. I wouldn't be missing you so much, Mum.

Tan

My baby's father wants the baby to tan like I do. He doesn't want it to burn in the sun like he does. I want it to heal like he does—this baby does not deserve blemishes, scarring. All babies deserve perfection. I want this baby to have its father's ears, eyes, beautiful even teeth, blond hair and calming inner beauty. It glows and everybody can see it within him. It makes me the darker, less safe of the two. I wish for the baby to be a girl. It already has my long chicken legs. My skin thins as it stretches and reveals the purple sinewy muscles beneath. We watch the outline of its feet as it flexes within. We both want this baby to have the culmination of our love because that is what it is, symbolically. I think grandparents merely need to see it draw breath.

Some relatives have asked if it was likely to come out 'dark'. I raged quietly at the source of the question. It was implied that it would be lovely if it came out 'dark'. We said given my Aboriginal and his Irish heritage, it was likely to come out as black as coal with a shock of red hair.

There is a picture in a laundry somewhere of children running. The last child is Aboriginal and his nappy has fallen down. He holds on to it, trying to keep up with the other white children. The title says, 'The little black behind'.

I itch to take down that picture and throw it into the washing machine. Smash it in the spin cycle and wash it all away

Mum

I don't care about the colour of my baby. Maybe I should. I care that it gets to know you, Mum. It will need to, to balance out all its other relatives, me included. I know I can only protect it so much. I know I can't even protect it from myself, my body, my blood. The hospital testifies to that. At the very least it plays on my genetic inadequacies and my undeniable sense of guilt. All I can do is rage against the system and call on the strengths of my collective heritage. I cannot reject myself so I'm rallying all ranks in this war, even my generals. That is why I think I really miss you, Mum. Can't say any of this on the telephone.

Wind Change

At night the air is sweet and cool. If the wind is blowing the right way. Now it is blowing from the sea. Not from the concrete factory. But the wind might change as we sleep and we might wake to the smell of dog shit. The suburbs.

Water

A gush between the legs.

'Hon, could you get up and check.' It's two in the morning. He grunts, sits up and wanders around the bed.

He turns on the light, and I bury my head in the pillow. Steeling myself, I look at his face. He is looking at my opening, from a distance though, as the water gushes forth.

I feel removed, floating away.

'It's the water. It's broken . . . I think.'

'Oh . . .' The mattress soaks and sags. 'I'd better get up then.'

Lever myself up. He hands me a towel, water splashing onto the floorboards as I walk. Wondering vaguely if it will eat away the polish. 'Must clean it up,' I think. But I'm in no condition. I sit on the toilet and hear the water flushing down. 'It doesn't feel right . . . I want to save it.'

I lean over the bath, put the plug in and sit on the edge, listening to the splash, the pooling of water.

'There's no blood.' I'm surprised by its clarity. Pale wine. 'I'm a grape . . .'

When the pains come I plug the gushing with a towel and leave for the hospital. In the car I wait as the seconds pass on the grandfather watch. Like a swimmer timing my own race and I breathe a six-beat kick with each contraction.

'We are not going to name it Clarence. If it's a boy I'm naming it Tristan,' I pant.

'After the bloke in "All Creatures Great and Small"?' He waits for the contraction to pass. 'Yeah? Well, that's a crap name.' He offers me some water.

'Yes.' Grunt. 'Breathe, Breathe,' I whisper to myself. Manage to walk into the hospital. An ambulance driver taking a smoke-o says, 'I can tell you've done this sort of thing before.' He drags deeply on his cigarette and blows it up into the night sky.

I want to say, 'No, I haven't,' but I find myself strapped on a bed waiting to be measured from the inside out. And besides, someone is still arguing the point.

A nurse says, 'Do you mind if I keep my hand in during the next contraction?' and doesn't wait for an answer.

Fuck this for a joke, but I'm too polite to say it out loud. Delirium sets in. I say to the nurse, 'Nola? Is your name really Nola? That's my mother's name. That's a good sign. Can I get up now?'

'We're not naming it Nola.' A voice drones through the fluorescent lighting. His voice.

'Well, you don't like Neil or Finn. Oooooh.' Another contraction comes and the room warps with the pain.

'Nurse? She's not making sense,' he says. I'm beginning to shake.

The nurse rubs my back. 'Her body has gone into shock.'

'Shock?'

'It hasn't been in labour before.'

'Neither have I,' I pant. 'I want to get into the bath and I want it hot!'

Clamber into the bath. Halfway over the side a contraction comes. 'Ooooh, oh god, oh god.'

'It's alright. It will be finished soon,' says the nurse.

I push myself over and slide under the tap. 'That's better.'

'You want some water, honey-bun?' He offers me a glass. Bloody tap water. Water from the tap that comes from the river. I can taste the river and the glass on my lips and I gag.

'No—stop breathing.' Push the glass away. Hold the bath.

'Stop breathing?' he asks.

'Yes. I said STOP BREATHING!' The contraction lulls. 'It's annoying me.'

Another contraction comes. 'Nurse, I want to push.'

'Let me check.' And she puts on a glove.

'Can I have some gas? Please? Now! I want some gas now! Now! Please.'

'Nurse, did you hear that? She wants me to stop breathing?' The nurse smiles at him.

'Just move away. Just get away. Oh god!'

'Just breathe the gas in, nice and deep, that's right.'

'I can't do this.'

'Yes, yes, you can, honey-bun.'

Chants between gasps. 'Earth my body, water my blood, AIR MY BREATH and fire my spirit.' Each contraction makes me louder and louder. The contractions start squeezing thick and fast.

'Talk to me! Talk to me!' I scream at him.

He searches for words. He's never seen her like this before. 'Do you remember when we went to the beach?'

'WHAT BEACH?' Sucking in the gas now. My face is pressed hard into the mask.

'We went swimming. Remember, think about Yamba.'

'FUCK FUCKING YAMBA!'

The midwife arrives. 'That's good,' she says. 'Swearing is good.'

'Think about your Nana. Think about her strength.'

'Oh Nana,' I sob. 'Oh Nana, I can't do this. Help me!' I take another gasp of the gas. I feel that the front of my pelvic bone will split.

'Ooh look. There's blood floating in my bath.' Another gasp of gas. 'Whose blood is that?' I ask the midwife. 'They should've washed the bath out before I got in.' Sharp intake of breath. 'I WANT TO PUSH NOW! I want to push!'

'You are not ready yet. You're not fully dilated.'

'I want to push!' I bear down, into the water, gripping the bath. I am greeted by a sharp pain, a sledgehammer smashing me inside.

A woman in the next room is screaming, 'I want to die. Help me! Help me! I'm dying!'

The midwife looks uncomfortable. 'Sorry about that.'

'Sorry about what?' More chanting, 'I am dilating, I am dilating. Oh god! I can't do this any more.'

'C'mon, honey. The little sucker's just gonna slip right out.'

Outside the hospital a heatwave has broken onto the city. Forty degrees perhaps. Inside the labour ward it is like a fridge. Slide out of the bath onto the floor. Cold, wet, shivering uncontrollably, I crawl on the carpet.

'Like my mother and her mother before me,' I sob to the carpet, 'Nana, dolphins, anybody. Give me drugs! Please.' A frozen icepick goes through my back. I shove my face into a pillow and scream.

'Please, I'm sorry I failed. I can't do this. Just give me an epidural.'

Outside the door the midwife says, 'We'll give her another half-hour.'

'Yeah, okay,' he says.

Another contraction.

'Get me out! Get me out!' Delirious, chanting, 'I am opening my cervix. My cervix is opening. The remaining lip has dissolved. I am opening. I am progressing well. The baby is not distressed. The baby is relaxed, waiting to come out. What would Nana have done?' Another contraction. Waves breaking over this body, smashing it apart. I'm the pain, I'm the unwanted union between the sea and the beach. Keep chanting. 'The baby and I are at one with the universe. The baby and I are one!' Another contraction. 'I'm sorry. I'm sorry!' Breathe, breathe. 'We are relaxed enough to birth. We are ready. We are preparing ourselves. We greet this birth joyfully, openly.' Whispering, 'My cervix is awash with life-giving light, buttercup yellow, pale amber. Opening to the universe.' More pain. The midwife examines me.

I'm sobbing, 'Oh Nana, I'm sorry. I've done something wrong.'

'The cervix is not effacing. The baby is stuck. We'll transfer you now—poor dear.'

Another contraction. Yell into the carpet. 'I AM A CHILD OF THE UNIVERSE!'

Bloodied contractions. Haemorrhaging bladder. Caesarean section. Child of the universe. Universal cut, slash me open, reveal my child. Throw her up to the sky.

Child

The first breath, splitting her lungs open like a gunshot love, is borne. She is a girl. Small, pink like a splitting rose bud. The little purple body turns coral pink and she gives a yell of indignation. She tries to kick the hospital staff away. She wants to burrow back to where she has come from.

Empty

A week later we come home.

I check on the bath. It is white, empty. There is a faint grittiness from the cleaner. Sit in the bath.

'I've lost my water.' I stare at the plug.

'Honey?' He walks in to see me sitting in the empty bath. He is gentle with me. 'What are you doing, honey-bun?'

'I don't know. Where have I all gone?'

He puts in the plug, turns on the tap, kisses my forehead. 'It's alright, hon, you're all here. You're home.' He leaves to check on the baby.

Lean forward, touch the tap. 'Fill me up,' I say but no one can hear me over the roar of the water from the river.

The baby sleeps softly in the scent of powder. Talc

and milk mix. I breathe the talc in and think, 'It is like a memory, filling your mind at the wrong time. Making you lonely for something you can't have.'

Later, I can walk in and turn on the tap without thinking, without looking. The floorboards gleam, and the baby giggles at her own reflection.

We can sit and play in the water.

Smile and sigh under the baby's weight.

'This is not your first splash my girl, my Ashlyn May,' I say.

My baby giggles and kicks at the scar she left behind.

My Ashlyn May

We all have our journeys, our stories, don't we? Ones we want to keep, ones we want to share. Distractions from the present day, flying from the past, worries about the future. It's all there as we walk around in our head, in our bodies.

You are running now. It's taken me that long to write this down. To sort the emotions and blood from the dust. Things have melted and reformed in my life. You are pale, like your father. You have red hair and blue eyes.

I've thrown off some of the boundaries I thought were my identity. I've kept all the memories I could find.

We come from a land of rivers and dust, of markings made by people of clay. Only the forms and the names change.

Your mother is not here though. I am of the dispossessed. So are you. We are another generation removed from our land, from our Dreaming. Yet we walk on this continent and we remember while rivers and dust flow in our blood.

No one can define who we are but ourselves.

The colour of your ancestors' clay has faded, but see your hair shine in our sun.

$\mathcal{A}cknowledgements$

I'd like to thank the following people for all of their help and assistance.

Firstly, thank you Annette Barlow, Emily O'Connell, Julia Stiles, Colette Vella and Christa Munns for the editorial encouragement and opportunity to have this book published. I still can't quite believe it.

Secondly, most of the research into this manuscript would not have been done without a research grant funded by the Australia Council. This grant was awarded for new or aspiring writers during the death throes of a Keating Labor government. It was then axed under the Howard regime and 'aspiring' writers now need to publish three novels to qualify for a similar grant. I just love a country where everybody gets a fair go. So, thanks again, Australia Council. The financial report's in the mail.

A special mention to Bruce Pascoe who, whenever

I needed a confidence boost, gave me timely, succinct and straightforward constructive criticism instead.

To Olga Gostin, my 'primary' editor, who taught me the meaning of the words 'draft', 're-submit' and 'bloody perfectionist'.

Bits and pieces of this manuscript have been published previously. 'Public Notice' and 'Fractals in the Landscape' have seen the light of day in *Australian Short Stories, No. 55*, Pascoe Publishing, Apollo Bay (1996), and *Across Country: Stories from Aboriginal Australia*, ABC Books, Sydney, 1998.

I would also like to acknowledge material used from the following publications: *Frontier* by Henry Reynolds, Allen & Unwin, Sydney, 1987 (excerpts on pp. 92, 95–7); *A Secret Country* by John Pilger, Random House, Sydney, 1990 (excerpt on p. 93); 'Rivers of Blood' by Rory Medcalf, adapted from a series published in *The Northern Star*, 1989 (excerpts on pp. 92–5); 'Me and You' by Della Walker, AIATSIS (excerpt on p. 161); 'Isle of the Vanishing Men, Stone Age to the 20th Century', extract from *The Daily Examiner*, 1936 (excerpt on p. 161); 'Bundjalung Settlement and Migration' by Margaret Sharpe, *Aboriginal History* (9), 1985 (excerpt on pp. 163–4); *A History of Yamba and Iluka* by Eleanor McSwan, Clarence Press, 1978 (excerpt on p. 165).

To my friends and family who argued with and encouraged me while I had a couple of kids and wrote this book, especially:

Nola Boland. Thank you for teaching me to 'sit down, shut up and write'. I love you Mum.

Ken Boland. Thanks for putting up with all of my crap and being there for Mum, Ken.

My beautiful, intelligent, funny sisters Sandra Bayet and Jacqui Boland.

Uncle Mark, Sandy and Sam Williams. Heroes.

David Shelton and Mandy Williamson; Nick Tabart; Dianne Barrett and John Henderson for their sympathetic ears and guidance when I need it.

Sarah-Jane Cook—'Shum'. The Greek goddess with the camera in her hand. Yeah, that's her.

'Aunty Lisa-la' Newchglod. Thank you for helping me survive Dad's death and the year 2000.

Also, this book would not have been edited without the unconditional love and coffee from Mylor Café.

Finally, to my babes—Ashlyn May Charlton and Cedar David Charlton. I'd start writing how much I love them but you'd never shut me up.

$\mathcal{S}ources$

Australian Institute of Aboriginal and Torres Strait Islander Studies (AIATSIS, ACT): Caldwell, Florence, 'Mrs Florence Caldwell, Executive Member of APA, Writes Her Story for "Churinga" ', Churinga, APA, July 1965–May 1971, p 19.

AIATSIS: Heron, Ronald, 'Aboriginal Perspectives: an ethnohistory of six Aboriginal Communities', 1991.

AIATSIS: Holmer, Nils M, 'Stories from Two Native Tribes of Eastern Australia', *Australian Essays and Studies*, 1969.

AIATSIS: Extract from *The Daily Examiner* (Grafton), 13 June 1936, 'Isle of the Vanishing Men, Stone Age to the 20th Century: Ulgundahi settlement makes people happy', Maclean District Historical Society, 1980.

AIATSIS: Keats, NC, 'Woollumbin: the creation and early habitation of the Tweed, Brunswick and Richmond Rivers of New South Wales', 1990.

AIATSIS: Mathews, Robert Hamilton, 'Folk-lore of the Australian Aborigines', *Science of Man* (1).

AIATSIS: McSwan, Eleanor H, *A History of Yamba and Iluka*, Clarence Press, 1978 and *Maclean: The First Fifty Years, 1862–1912*, 1992.

AIATSIS: Prentis, Malcolm David, 'Aborigines and Europeans in the Northern Area of New South Wales, 1823–1881'.

AIATSIS: Walker, Della, 'Me and You'.

Archives Office of New South Wales, 'Re: School for Aborigines at Ulgundahi Island', Police Station Maclean, 30 April 1908, pp. 1–5.

Lamshed, Max, 'First News from Science Camp, Natives Enthusiastic, Patient for all Tests, Plaster Casts and Black Barber', *Advertiser*, 13 August 1932, Adelaide, p 32.

Medcalf, Rory, 'Rivers of Blood: massacres of the Northern Rivers Aborigines and their resistance to the white occupation, 1838–1870', adapted from a series published in *The Northern Star*, 1989.

Pilger, John, *A Secret Country*, Random House, Sydney, 1990.

Reynolds, Henry, *Dispossession*, Allen & Unwin, Sydney, 1989.

Reynolds, Henry, *Frontier*, Allen & Unwin, Sydney, 1987.

Robinson, Roland, *Aboriginal Myths and Legends*, Sun Books, Melbourne, 1966.

Sharpe, Margaret C, 'Bundjalung Settlement and Migration', *Aboriginal History* (9), 1985.

Sharpe, Margaret C, 'Mr Tindale's Patience', *The Advertiser*, 13 August 1932, p. 32.